ENGLISH GRAMMAR
FOR
STUDENTS OF ITALIAN

SERGIO ADORNI
KAREN PRIMORAC

UNIVERSITY OF WINDSOR

The Olivia and Hill Press, Inc.
P.O. Box 7396
Ann Arbor, Michigan 48107

English Grammar series
edited by Jacqueline Morton

English Grammar for Students of French, 2nd edition
English Grammar for Students of Spanish, 2nd edition
English Grammar for Students of German, 2nd edition
English Grammar for Students of Italian
English Grammar for Students of Latin
English Grammar for Students of Russian

Printed in the U.S.A.

Library of Congress Catalog Card Number: 82-80515

ISBN 0-934034-04-4

10 9 8 7 6

Contents

Preface

English Grammar for Students of Italian is a simple, practical, self-study manual written to aid high school, college and university students who are beginning the study of Italian. It is patterned after the popular *English Grammar for Students of French* by Jacqueline Morton and follows similar handbooks for students of Spanish, German and Latin. It is not meant to be comprehensive nor is it designed to replace textbooks of Italian, but rather to supplement them and make them more accessible. Students can, of course, speak and write their own native English without a conscious knowledge of grammar. Nevertheless, as they begin the study of a second language, they inevitably lose their way in a maze of grammatical terms and structures, which many of them may be encountering for the first time.

The main purpose of this manual is to help students to overcome this lack of formal knowledge by providing them with the basic elements of grammar which they can then apply to their study of Italian. In plain and simple language, *English Grammar for Students of Italian* defines terms such as "indirect object," "past participle," "relative pronoun" and then compares and contrasts their forms and functions in English and Italian, pointing out the major similarities and differences between the two languages. In order to simplify the presentation, certain key English and Italian structures are analyzed point-by-point and clarified by easy-to-read charts, while those which are complex and which have no English equivalent have been only briefly mentioned. For example, the treatment of the subjunctive and complex details of pronouns are left almost entirely to the Italian textbook.

This handbook covers most of the material presented in textbooks of beginning Italian and uses their conventional terminology. It contains 48 chapters, each of which may be studied as a separate entity but which can also be easily related to the others by extensive cross-references and by a carefully itemized index.

Teachers may wish to use in class the many examples and contrastive analyses presented in the manual. They may also assign specific sections as supplements to particular homework assignments, since the manual can be easily keyed to any elementary textbook. The instructor likewise will discover that use of the manual not only saves time in lesson preparation, but also frees valuable class time which can then be devoted to language practice.

We would like to thank Ana Besne for her competent preparation of the typescript and Donald Waddell for his helpful comments on the manuscript. We would also like to acknowledge our indebtedness to Jacqueline Morton for her valuable suggestions and painstaking efforts in reorganizing parts of the book.

S.A.
K.P.

Introduction

In order to learn a foreign language, in this case Italian, you must look at every word in three ways: you must be aware of each word's meaning, class, and use.

1. MEANING of the word—You learn new vocabulary in Italian by memorizing each new word and its English equivalent.

The English word *book* has the same meaning as Italian **libro.**

Sometimes two words are the same or very similar in both English and Italian. These are called COGNATES. They are especially easy to learn.

English	Italian
intelligent	intelligente
student	studente
to continue	continuare
dentist	dentista

Sometimes knowing one Italian word will help you learn another.

Knowing that **bambino** is *boy* should help you learn that **bambina** is *girl;* or knowing that **latte** means *milk* should help you to learn that **lattaio** means *milkman.*

But generally there is little similarity between words, and knowing one Italian word will not help you to learn another. Therefore, you must learn each vocabulary item separately.

Knowing that **uomo** means *man* will not help you learn that **donna** means *woman.*

Moreover, sometimes words in combination will take on a special meaning.

In Italian **fare** means *to make;* **coda** means *tail.* However **fare la coda** means *to line up.*

Such an expression, which has a meaning as a whole different from the combined meaning of the individual words in it, is called an IDIOM. For instance, when we say in English "They threw the book at him" we are not really talking about throwing books but rather we are expressing the idea that someone received a severe penalty. Be careful not to turn English idioms word for word into Italian, for example "to have a good time" is not ***avere un buon tempo,** but **divertirsi.** You will need to pay special attention to idioms in order to recognize them and use them correctly.

2. CLASS of the word—English and Italian words are classified according to PART OF SPEECH. We shall consider eight different parts of speech:

noun	verb
pronoun	adverb
adjective	preposition
article	conjunction

Each part of speech has its own rules for use. You must learn to identify the part of speech to which a word belongs in order to choose the correct Italian equivalent and use it correctly in a sentence.

In your dictionary, the part of speech is always given in italics right after the word entry. If you look up *student,* you will find *student, n.* (noun); if you look up *beautiful,* you will find *beautiful, adj.* (adjective), etc. However, a word may belong to more than one part of speech.

---

* An asterisk means that what follows is incorrect. It is merely an illustration.

Look at the word *that* in the following sentences:

     a. *That* girl is my sister.   (adjective)
     b. I don't believe *that.*   (pronoun)
     c. He was *that* smart   (adverb)
     d. He said *that* he was busy.   (conjunction)

The same word, *that,* represents four different parts of speech. You must recognize them in order to find the Italian equivalent where, in this case, a different word corresponds to each part of speech.

3. USE of the word—In addition to its classification as part of speech, each word has a special FUNCTION or use within a sentence. A noun or pronoun, for example, can be used as a subject, direct object, indirect object, or object of a preposition. Determining the function of a word will help you choose the correct Italian form and know what rules apply.

Look at the word *him* in the following sentences:

     a. I don't know *him.*   (direct object)
     b. Have you told *him?*   (indirect object)
     c. Are you going with *him?*   (object of preposition)

In English the same word *him* has three different functions, but in Italian a different form of the pronoun will correspond to each function.

Note: As a student of Italian you must learn to recognize parts of speech and determine the use of words within a sentence. This is essential because in Italian words have a great deal of influence upon each other.

Compare the following sentence in English and Italian.

    *The small red **shoes** are under the small white box.*

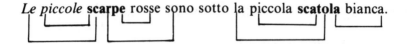

Le piccole **scarpe** rosse sono sotto la piccola **scatola** bianca.

In English: The only word that affects the form of another word in the sentence is *shoes*, which affects *are*. (If the word were *shoe, are* would be *is.)*

In Italian: The word for *shoes* **(scarpe)** affects not only the word for *are* **(sono)** but also the form of the words for *the* **(le),** *little* **(piccole),** and *red* **(rosse).**

The word for *box* **(scatola)** affects the words for *the* **(la),** *small* **(piccola),** and *white* **(bianca).**

The only word which is not affected is the word for *under,* **sotto.**

Since parts of speech and function are usually determined in the same way in English and Italian, this handbook will show you how to identify them in English. You will then learn to compare English and Italian constructions. This will give you a better understanding of the grammar explanations in your Italian textbook.

What is a Noun?

A NOUN is a word that names:

• a person	teacher, boy, Frank, Smith, friend
• a place	city, state, country, Rome, Italy
• a thing or animal	book, house, cat, water, duck
• an idea or quality	truth, beauty, peace, happiness, democracy

Nouns that always begin with a capital letter, such as the names of people and places (Mary Smith, Italy), are called PROPER NOUNS. Nouns that do not begin with a capital letter (house, bicycle, piano) are called COMMON NOUNS.

To help you to recognize nouns, here is a paragraph where the nouns are in italics:

Italy produces many agricultural, industrial and artistic *items* which are in *demand* throughout the *world*. The *cultivation* of the *grape* and the *olive* is of great *importance* to the Italian *economy* and many *countries* import fine Italian *wines* and olive[1] *oil*. Among the many industrial *exports* are *automobiles, typewriters,* sewing *machines* and electrical *appliances*. *Italy* is also famous for its *handicrafts;* among them leather[1] *goods* from *Florence, glassware* from *Venice,* coral[1] *jewelry* from *Naples,* and *ceramics* from *Faenza*. The *achievements* of Italian *artists* and *musicians* have been recognized for *centuries* and the *popularity* of Italian *fashion,* industrial *design* and *movies* extends far beyond the *borders* of the *country*.

---

[1]These are examples of a noun used as an adjective, that is, to describe another noun. See p. 107.

What is Meant by Gender?

When a word can be classified as to whether it is masculine, feminine, or neuter, it is said to have a GENDER.

Gender plays a very small role in English; however, since it is at the very heart of the Italian language, let us see what evidence of gender we have in English.

In English: Normally gender reflects the noun's biological sex; that is male beings are masculine, female beings are feminine. Objects and abstract ideas are neuter. When we use a noun we often do not realize that it has a gender. But when we replace the noun with *he, she,* or *it,* we choose only one of the three without hesitation because we automatically give a gender to the noun we are replacing.

The ***boy*** came home; ***he*** was tired, and I was glad to see ***him.***

A noun *(boy)* is of the MASCULINE GENDER if *he* or *him* is used to substitute for it.

My ***aunt*** came for a visit; ***she*** is nice and I like ***her.***

A noun *(aunt)* is of the FEMININE GENDER if *she* or *her* is used to substitute for it.

There is a ***tree*** in front of the house. ***It*** is a maple.

A noun *(tree)* is of the NEUTER GENDER if *it* is substituted for it.[1]

In Italian: All nouns are either masculine or feminine. Nouns indicating male beings are masculine and those indicating female beings are feminine. There are no neuter nouns. This means that

[1]There are a few well-known exceptions, such as *ship,* which is referred to as *she.* It is custom, not logic, which decides. "The S/S United States sailed for Europe. She is a good ship."

all nouns referring to objects or abstract ideas are either masculine or feminine. In this case gender is somewhat arbitrary and cannot be figured out in the same way as in English. Therefore you should pay special attention to the gender of these nouns.

Examples of English neuter nouns which have MASCULINE equivalents in Italian	Examples of English neuter nouns which have FEMININE equivalents in Italian
book	library
country	nation
vice	virtue
Canada	Italy
Monday	Sunday
sorrow	happiness
power	weakness

It is essential to know the gender of nouns since it influences other words in the sentence (articles, adjectives, pronouns).

Gender can usually be determined by looking at the ending of a noun. All Italian nouns, with a few exceptions, end in a vowel.

• nouns ending in **-o** are usually masculine

il libro	*book*
il giorno	*day*
il gatto	*cat*
il maestro	*teacher*

• nouns ending in **-a** are usually feminine

la carta	*paper*
la rosa	*rose*
la casa	*house*
la maestra	*teacher*

• nouns ending in **-e** can be masculine or feminine

When you encounter one of these nouns you will have to memorize it with its gender.

Masculine Nouns		Feminine Nouns	
il dottore	*doctor*	la lezione	*lesson*
il nome	*name*	la televisione	*television*
il giornale	*newspaper*	la capitale	*capital*
il signore	*gentleman*	la sete	*thirst*
il professore	*professor*	la voce	*voice*
il bicchiere	*glass*	la notte	*night*

There are a few exceptions to the above rules, for instance, **la mano** *(the hand)* is a feminine noun even though it ends in **-o; il problema** *(the problem)* is a masculine noun even though it ends in **-a.** Your textbook and instructor will point out the exceptions. When you are not sure, remember that the gender of a noun is always indicated in an Italian dictionary. Also, whenever a definite or indefinite article is used with a noun, the article usually indicates the gender of the noun. (See **What are Indefinite and Definite Articles?, p. 12.**)

What is Meant by Number?

NUMBER is the designation of a word as singular or plural. When a word refers to one person or thing, it is said to be SINGULAR; when it refers to more than one, it is called PLURAL.

In English: Nouns, pronouns and verbs are the parts of speech which have number, i.e., which have a singular and plural form.

- I read the *book.*
  |
  noun
  singular

  I read the *books.*
  |
  noun
  plural

- *I* read the book.
  |
  pronoun
  singular

  They read the book.
  |
  pronoun
  plural

See **What is a Subject Pronoun?**, p. 32.

- I *am* reading the book.
  |
  verb
  singular

They *are* reading the book.
|
verb
plural

See **What is a Verb Conjugation?**, p. 37.

In this section we will talk only about the number of nouns.

We indicate the plural of nouns in several ways:

● most commonly by adding an *-s* or *-es* to a singular noun

book ⎯⎯⎯⎯⎯➤ book*s*
kiss ⎯⎯⎯⎯⎯➤ kiss*es*

● sometimes by making a spelling change

man ⎯⎯⎯⎯➤ m*en*
leaf ⎯⎯⎯⎯➤ lea*ves*
child ⎯⎯⎯⎯➤ child*ren*

Some nouns, called COLLECTIVE NOUNS, refer to a group of persons or things, but they are considered singular.

A football *team* has eleven players.
The *family* is well.
The *crowd* was under control.

In Italian: Nouns, pronouns, verbs, articles, and adjectives are the parts of speech which have number. It is important that you be able to identify a word as singular or plural because the number of one word will often influence the number of another. Moreover, a word in the plural is spelled and pronounced differently from its singular form.

In this section we will talk only about the number of nouns.

Nouns which end in

● **-o** or **-e** change to **-i** to form the plural

libro	⟶ libri	*book*	⟶ *books*
ragazzo	⟶ ragazzi	*boy*	⟶ *boys*
giornale	⟶ giornali	*newspaper*	⟶ *newspapers*
lezione	⟶ lezioni	*lesson*	⟶ *lessons*

A final **-i** does not always indicate a masculine plural noun. Remember the example **la lezione** ⟶ **le lezioni** *(the lesson, the lessons)* which is a feminine plural noun.

● **-a** change to **-e** to form the plural

casa	⟶ case	*house*	⟶ *houses*
ragazza	⟶ ragazze	*girl*	⟶ *girls*

● a vowel with a written accent or in a consonant do not change to form the plural

città	⟶ città	*city*	⟶ *cities*
virtù	⟶ virtù	*virtue*	⟶ *virtues*
bar	⟶ bar	*bar*	⟶ *bars*
film	⟶ film	*film*	⟶ *films*

Your textbook will point out exceptions to these three basic rules.

Note: Nouns do not change gender when they become plural.

What are Indefinite and Definite Articles?

The ARTICLE is a word placed before a noun to indicate if the noun refers to an unspecified person, animal or object or if the noun refers to a particular person, animal or object.

In English:

A. Indefinite Articles

We use *a* or *an* before a noun when we are not speaking of a particular person, animal or object. They are called INDEFINITE ARTICLES.

> I saw *a* boy in the street.
>
> not a particular boy

> I ate *an* apple.
>
> not a particular apple

The indefinite article is used only with a singular noun; if the noun becomes plural, either the indefinite article is omitted or it is replaced by the word *some.*

> I saw boys in the street
> I saw *some* boys in the street.

> I ate apples.
> I ate *some* apples.

B. Definite Articles

We use *the* before a noun when we are speaking of a particular person, animal or object. It is called the DEFINITE ARTICLE.

I saw *the* boy you spoke to me about.

a particular boy

I ate *the* apple you gave me.

a particular apple

The definite article remains *the* when the noun becomes plural.

I saw *the boys* you spoke to me about.

I ate *the apples* you gave me.

In Italian: The article, indefinite or definite, has a much greater role than its English equivalent. It works hand in hand with the noun it belongs to by matching the noun's gender and number. This "matching" is called AGREEMENT. One says that "the article agrees with the noun." You use a different article depending on whether the noun is masculine or feminine, and depending on whether the noun is singular or plural. (See **What is Meant by Gender?**, p. 6 and **What is Meant by Number?**, p. 9.)

A. Indefinite articles

- **un** indicates a masculine singular noun

| un libro | *a book* |
| un ragazzo | *a boy* |

  uno indicates a masculine singular noun which begins with a **z-** or an **s** + consonant

| uno zio | *an uncle* |
| uno studente | *a student* |

- **una** indicates a feminine singular noun

| una casa | *a house* |
| una ragazza | *a girl* |

un' indicates a feminine singular noun which begins with a vowel

un' automobile	*an automobile*
un' amica	*a girl friend*

The indefinite article is used only with a singular noun; if the noun becomes plural, in Italian it is preceded by the partitive (see **What is a Partitive?**, p. 17).

B. <u>Definite articles</u>

• **il** indicates a masculine singular noun

il libro	*the book*
il ragazzo	*the boy*

lo indicates a masculine singular noun which begins with a **z-** or an **s** + consonant

lo zio	*the uncle*
lo studente	*the student*

l' indicates a masculine singular noun which begins with a vowel

l'anno	*the year*
l'orologio	*the watch*

• **la** indicates a feminine singular noun

la casa	*the house*
la ragazza	*the girl*

l' indicates a feminine singular noun which begins with a vowel

l'idea	*the idea*
l'alba	*the dawn*

● **i** indicates a masculine plural noun

i libri	*the books*
i ragazzi	*the boys*

gli indicates a masculine plural noun which begins with either **z-** or **s** + consonant, or a vowel

gli studenti	*the students*
gli anni	*the years*

● **le** indicates a feminine plural noun

le case	*the houses*
le ragazze	*the girls*

Learn nouns with their singular definite article; the article will show if the noun is masculine or feminine[1].

---

[1]The only exception: nouns which begin with a vowel, for example **l'amico** *(the boy friend),* **l'amica** *(the girl friend).* Here the **-o** or **-a** ending of the noun clearly indicates its gender. But the gender of nouns with **-e** ending must be memorized:

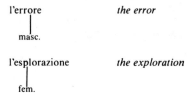

l'errore   *the error*

masc.

l'esplorazione   *the exploration*

fem.

It may help to learn these nouns ending in **-e** with their indefinite article:

un errore   un'esplorazione

masc.   fem.

Here is a chart you can use as reference:

Noun begins with:	Definite Articles				Indefinite Articles	
	Masculine		Feminine		Masculine	Feminine
	Sing.	Pl.	Sing.	Pl.	Sing.	Sing.
1. vowel	l'	gli	l'	le	un	un'
2. z or s + consonant	lo	gli	la	le	uno	una
3. other consonant	il	i	la	le	un	una

The definite article is used much more frequently in Italian than in English.

> **La** guerra è terribile.
> *War is terrible.*

> Quella donna è **la** signora Bianchi.
> *That woman is Mrs. Bianchi.*

> **I** turisti sono bene accolti in Italia.
> *Tourists are well received in Italy.*

Your textbook will instruct you on the uses of the indefinite and definite articles.

What is a Partitive?

A PARTITIVE indicates that only part of a whole (*some* bread, *some* water) or part of a group of things or people (*some* letters, *some* boys) is being referred to.

In English: The idea of the partitive is normally expressed with *some* or *any,* although these words are often dropped.

> He is buying (some) bread.
> She drank (some) water.
> I saw (some) boys on the street.
> I don't have (any) friends here.

In Italian: The partitive is normally expressed by the preposition **di** combined with the definite article. (See **What is a Preposition?**, p. 130 and **What are Indefinite and Definite Articles?**, p. 12.)

$$
\text{di} + \begin{cases}
\text{il} & \longrightarrow \text{del} \\
\text{lo} & \longrightarrow \text{dello} \\
\text{l'} & \longrightarrow \text{dell'} \\
\text{la} & \longrightarrow \text{della} \\
\text{i} & \longrightarrow \text{dei} \\
\text{gli} & \longrightarrow \text{degli} \\
\text{le} & \longrightarrow \text{delle}
\end{cases}
$$

Although the partitive words *some* or *any* may be dropped in English, the partitive cannot be left out in Italian, except in interrogative (see p. 47) and negative sentences (see p. 45).

● Compra **del** pane.

   di + il

He is buying (some) bread.

- Ha bevuto **dell'**acqua.

  └─ di + l'

  She drank (some) water.

- Ho visto **dei** ragazzi per strada.

  └─ di + i

  I saw (some) boys on the street.

But:

Hai amici qui?
Do you have (any) friends here?

Non ho amici qui.
I don't have (any) friends here.

What is the Possessive?

The POSSESSIVE indicates the relationship of one noun to another in terms of possession or ownership.

In English: You can show possession in one of two ways:

1. With an APOSTROPHE

   - by adding APOSTROPHE + *s* to a singular possessor

     > John *'s* shirt
     > the girl *'s* dress
     > the boy *'s* shirt

   - by adding an APOSTROPHE to a plural possessor

     > the girls' father
     > the boys' team

2. With the word OF

   - by putting OF before a singular proper name

     > the shirt *of* John

   - by putting OF THE before another noun possessor

     > the dress *of the* girl
     > the shirt *of the* boy
     > the father *of the* girls
     > the team *of the* boys

In Italian: There is only one way to express possession and that is by using **di** *(of)* often combined with the definite article before the noun possessor (for the forms, see p. 17). Therefore, when you want to express the possessive, you must change the structure as this chart shows.

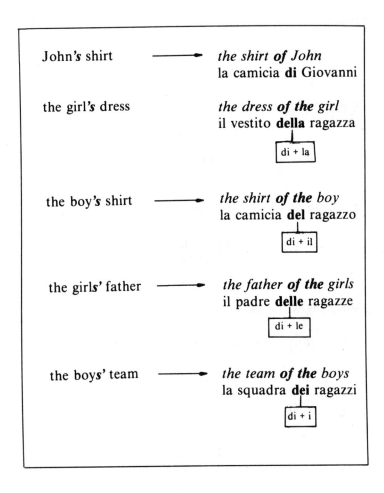

What is a Verb?

A VERB is a word that indicates an action, mental state or condition. The action can be physical, as in such verbs as *run, walk, hit, sit,* or mental, as in such verbs as *dream, think, believe,* and *hope.*

The verb is the most important element of a sentence, and you cannot express a complete thought (i.e., write a COMPLETE SENTENCE) without a verb.

To help you learn to recognize verbs, here is a paragraph where the verbs are in italics:

The three students **entered** the restaurant, **selected** a table, **hung** up their coats and **sat** down. They **looked** at the menu and **asked** the waitress what she **recommended.** She **advised** the daily special, beef stew. It **was** not expensive. They **chose** a bottle of red wine and **ordered** a salad. The service **was** slow, but the food **tasted** excellent. Good cooking, they **decided, takes** time. They **ordered** pastry for dessert and **finished** the meal with coffee.

A TRANSITIVE VERB is a verb that takes a direct object (see **What are Objects?,** p. 138). It is indicated by a *(v.t.)* in the dictionary.

The boy *threw* the ball.   to throw—transitive verb
       |
    direct object

She *quit* her job.   to quit—transitive verb
     |
  direct object

An INTRANSITIVE VERB is a verb that does not take a direct object. It is indicated by *(v.i.)* in the dictionary.

Paul *is sleeping.*   to sleep—intransitive verb
She *arrives* today.   to arrive—intransitive verb
       |
    adverb

Many verbs can be used transitively or intransitively, depending on whether they have a direct object in the sentence or not.

The students *speak* Italian.   to speak—transitive verb
direct object

Actions speak *louder* than words.   to speak—intransitive verb
adverb

In English: It is possible to modify the meaning of a verb by placing prepositions (see **What is a Preposition?**, p. 130) after it. The verb + preposition is called a PREPOSITIONAL VERB.

to look *for*	I *am looking for* a book.
to look *after*	I *look after* children.
to look *into*	He will *look into* it.
to look *at*	*Look at* that car.

In Italian: Usually a simple verb translates the meaning of an English prepositional verb. You will have to use an entirely different verb for each of these prepositional verbs.

cercare	*to look for*
badare	*to look after*
investigare	*to look into*
guardare	*to look at*

When looking up an English verb in the dictionary:

1. Check the English sentence to see if the verb is a prepositional verb or not.

2. If it is, make sure that you look up the specific meaning of the prepositional verb.

Never use the Italian equivalent of the simple verb (i.e. *look*) followed by the Italian equivalent of the preposition (i.e. *for, after, into, at*).

What is an Infinitive?

An INFINITIVE is a form of a verb. It can be considered the name of the verb; it is the form of the verb found in the dictionary as the main entry. The infinitive can never be used as the main verb of a sentence; there must always be another verb with it.

In English: The infinitive is usually composed of two words, TO + VERB: *to walk, to think, to be, to listen*. When you look up a verb in a dictionary you find it under the PLAIN INFINITIVE, that is the infinitive without the *to: walk, think, be, listen*. In a sentence, the infinitive is used with a conjugated verb. (See **What is a Verb Conjugation?**, p. 37.)

John and Mary *want to dance* together.
            main verb   infinitive

It *started to rain.*
   main verb   infinitive

24

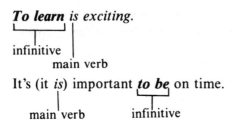

To learn is exciting.

infinitive

main verb

It's (it *is*) important *to be* on time.

main verb   infinitive

In Italian: The infinitive is composed of only one word which ends in **-are, -ere,** or **-ire.**

cant**are**	*to sing*
vend**ere**	*to sell*
part**ire**	*to leave*

You could say that the infinitive endings **(-are, -ere, -ire)** stand for "to" in English, while the initial part of the infinitive (THE STEM) carries the meaning of the word. In the case of the infinitive **cantare:**

cant-are   *to sing*

sing to

In a sentence the infinitive form is always used when a verb depends upon another verb which is not one of the auxiliary verbs, **essere** or **avere.** (See **What are Auxiliary Verbs?,** p. 26.)

- Giovanni e Maria vogliono **ballare** insieme.

infinitive

*John and Mary want **to dance** together.*

- Cominciò a **piovere.**

infinitive

*It started **to rain.***

• So **nuotare.**
     |
  infinitive

*I can **swim.***

• Dovresti **studiare** di più.
      |
   infinitive

*You should **study** more.*

Notice that in the last two examples English uses a plain infinitive (there is no "to") and that Italian uses an infinitive.

What are Auxiliary Verbs?

A verb is called an AUXILIARY VERB or HELPING VERB when it helps another verb form one of its tenses (see **What is Meant by Tense?**, p. 50). When it is used alone, it functions as a main verb.

Mary *is* a girl.	*is*	main verb
Paul *has* a headache.	*has*	main verb
They *go* to the movies.	*go*	main verb
They **have** *gone* to the movies.	**have**	auxiliary verb
	gone	main verb
His wife **has been** *gone* for two months.	**has**	auxiliary verb
	been	auxiliary verb
	gone	main verb

In English: There are many auxiliary verbs. They have two main uses:

1. to help formulate questions

Bob *has* a dog.	*has*	main verb
Does Bob *have* a dog?	**does**	auxiliary verb
	have	main verb
They *talked* on the phone.	*talked*	main verb
Did they *talk* on the phone?	**did**	auxiliary verb
	talk	main verb

2. to indicate the tense of the main verb (present, future, past—see **What is Meant by Tense?**, p. 50.)

Mary *is* reading a book.	Present
Mary *was* reading a book.	Past
Mary *will* read a book.	Future

In Italian: The two most important auxiliary verbs are **avere** *(to have)* and **essere** *(to be)*. (For the rules of their usage, see **What is the Past Tense?**, p. 67.)

Il ragazzo **ha** mangiato la mela.
auxiliary   main verb
avere

*The boy **has** eaten the apple.*

La ragazza **è** andata al cinema.
auxiliary   main verb
essere

*The girl **has** gone to the movies.*

Since the other English auxiliary verbs such as *do, does, did, will* or *would* do not exist as separate words in Italian, you cannot translate them as such. In Italian the meaning conveyed by these auxiliary verbs is indicated by the last letters (THE ENDING) of the main verb. You will find more on this subject under the different tenses.

What is a Subject?

In a sentence the person or thing that performs the action is called the SUBJECT.[1] When you wish to find the subject of a sentence, always look for the verb first; then ask, *WHO?* OR *WHAT?* BEFORE THE VERB. The answer will be the subject.

John speaks Italian.

> *Who* speaks Italian?
> Answer: John.
> *John* is the singular subject.

Are John and Mary coming tonight?

> *Who* is coming tonight?
> Answer: John and Mary.
> *John and Mary* is the plural subject.

Train yourself to always ask the question to find the subject. Never assume a word is the subject because it comes first in the sentence. Subjects can be in many different places of a sentence as you can see in the following examples in which the **subject** is in boldface and the *verb* italicised:

Did **the game** *start* on time?
After playing for two hours, **John** *became* exhausted.
Looking in the mirror *was* a little **girl.**

Some sentences have more than one main verb; you have to find the subject of each verb.

The **boys** *were doing* the cooking while **Mary** *was setting* the table.

---

[1]The subject performs the action in an active sentence, but is acted upon in a passive sentence (see **What is Meant by Active and Passive Voice?**, p. 101).

Boys is the plural subject of *were doing.*
Mary is the singular subject of *was setting.*

In English and in Italian it is very important to find the subject of each verb and to make sure that the subject and verb agree; that is, you must choose the form of the verb which goes with the subject. (See **What is a Verb Conjugation?**, p. 37.)

What is a Pronoun?

A PRONOUN is a word used in place of one or more nouns. It may stand, therefore, for a person, place, thing or idea.

For instance, instead of repeating the proper noun "Paul" in the following two sentences, we would use a pronoun in the second sentence:

Paul likes to sing. *Paul* goes to practice every day.
Paul likes to sing. *He* goes to practice every day.

A pronoun can only be used to refer to someone or something that has already been mentioned. The word that the pronoun replaces is called the ANTECEDENT of the pronoun.

In the example above, the pronoun *he* refers to the proper noun *Paul. Paul* is the antecedent of the pronoun *he.*

In English: There are different types of pronouns. They are studied in separate sections of this handbook. Below we will simply list the most important categories and refer you to the section where they are discussed in detail.

According to their function or their type, pronouns can be classified as follows:

- SUBJECT PRONOUNS (see p. 32)

    I go. *They* read. *He* runs.

- DIRECT OBJECT PRONOUNS (see p. 147)

    Paul loves *her*.
    Jane saw *them* at the theater.

- INDIRECT OBJECT PRONOUNS (see p. 150)

    The boy wrote *me* the letter.
    John gave *us* the book.

- OBJECT OF PREPOSITION PRONOUNS (see p. 152)

    Robert is going to the movies with *us*.
    He did it for *her*.

- REFLEXIVE PRONOUNS—These pronouns are used with reflexive verbs (see p. 98).

    I cut *myself*. We washed *ourselves*.

- INTERROGATIVE PRONOUNS—These pronouns are used in questions (see p. 157).

    Who is that? *What* do you want?

- **DEMONSTRATIVE PRONOUNS**—These pronouns are used to point out persons or things (see p. 163).

  This (one) is expensive. *That* (one) is cheap.

- **POSSESSIVE PRONOUNS**—These pronouns are used to show possession (see p. 167).

  Whose book is that? *Mine. Yours* is on the table.

- **RELATIVE PRONOUNS**—These pronouns are used to introduce relative subordinate clauses (see p. 169).

  The man *who* came is very nice.
  Mary, *whom* you met, is the president of the company.

In Italian: Pronouns are identified in the same way as in English. However, more often than in English, the pronoun agrees with the noun it replaces. That is, it must correspond in gender and in number with its antecedent.

What is a Subject Pronoun?

A SUBJECT PRONOUN is a pronoun used as a subject of a verb.

He worked while *she* read.

Who worked? Answer: He.
He is the subject of the verb *worked.*

Who read? Answer: She.
She is the subject of the verb *read.*

Subject pronouns are divided into groups accorded to the person speaking (the FIRST PERSON), the person spoken to (the SECOND PERSON), or the person spoken about (the THIRD PERSON). These groups are further divided according to singular or plural.

In Italian: The subject pronouns are used far less frequently than in English (see p. 44). Especially *it* and *they* referring to things are almost never used and should not be translated.

He has a new car.   *It is a Ferrari.*
Ha una macchina nuova.   È' una Ferrari.

She has many records.   *They are all new.*
Ha molti dischi.   Sono tutti nuovi.

Let us compare the subject pronouns of English and Italian.

English		Italian	
I	1st person singular the person speaking	io	
you	2nd person singular the person spoken to	tu	
he *she* *(it)*	3rd person singular person or thing spoken about by 1st and 2nd persons	lui lei	**Lei** [formal *you*]
we	1st person plural the person speaking plus others *John* and *I* speak Italian. ⌐————⌐ we	noi	
you	2nd person plural the persons spoken to	voi	
they	3rd person plural the persons or things spoken about by the 1st and 2nd persons	loro	**Loro** [formal *you*]

As you can see from the chart, there are two sets of pronouns for *you:* the familiar and the formal. **Tu, voi** are 2nd person pronouns; they are called FAMILIAR *YOU.* **Lei** and **Loro** are 3rd person pronouns and are called FORMAL *YOU.* To help you learn how to use the correct form, the following section has been devoted to "What is Meant by Familiar and Formal You?"

What is Meant by Familiar and Formal You?

In English: There is no difference between "you" in the singular and "you" in the plural. If you were in a room with many people and asked aloud "Are you coming with me?" the "you" could refer to one person or many; it could also refer to close friends or complete strangers.

In Italian: There is a difference between "you" in the singular and "you" in the plural; there is also a difference between the "you" used with close friends, the FAMILIAR *YOU*, and the "you" used with persons you do not know well, the FORMAL *YOU*.

A. FAMILIAR *YOU*

The familiar forms of *you* are used with members of one's family, friends, children and pets. In general, you use the familiar forms with persons you call by a first name.

● **tu**
                    familiar singular *you.*
                    It can refer to a male or female.

        Giovanni, **tu** vieni con me?
        *John, are **you** coming with me?*

        Maria, **tu** vieni con me?
        *Mary, are **you** coming with me?*

● **voi**
                    familiar plural *you.*
                    It refers to more than one person.

        Giovanni e Paolo, **voi** venite con me?
        *John and Paul, are **you** coming with me?*

        Giovanni e Maria, **voi** venite con me?
        *John and Mary, are **you** coming with me?*

B. FORMAL *YOU*

The formal forms of *you* are used to address persons you do not know well or persons to whom you should show respect. In general, you use the formal *you* with persons you address with a title: Miss Smith, Mr. Jones, Dr. Anderson, Professor Rossi.

● **Lei**   formal singular *you*.
                                   It can refer to a male or female.

    Signor Rossi, **Lei** viene con me?
    Mr. Rossi, are **you** *coming with me?*

    Signora Rossi, **Lei** viene con me?
    Mrs. Rossi, are **you** *coming with me?*

● **Loro**   formal plural *you*.
                                   It can refer to both males and females.

    Signori Rossi, **Loro** vengono con me?
    Mr. and Mrs. Rossi, are **you** *coming with me?*

    Signorine, **Loro** vengono con me?
    Young ladies, are **you** *coming with me?*

Note: The formal *you* words, **Lei** and **Loro,** are always written with a capital letter.

Remember that the same English sentence, "Are you coming with me?" can be said four different ways in Italian. This is a difficult concept for speakers of English and is especially important because it reflects the conventions of social relationships among Italian-speaking people. If you are in doubt as to whether to use the familiar or formal forms, use the formal forms unless speaking to a child or animal. The formal forms of *you* show respect for the person you are talking to and use of familiar forms can be considered rude if you do not know a person well.

Let's find the Italian equivalent for *you* in the following sentences.

- *Mr. President, are* **you** *coming with me?*

> Do you need familiar or formal forms? Formal.
> Is the *you* singular or plural? Singular.
> Then the form is **Lei.**

Signor Presidente, **Lei** viene con me?

- *Mr. and Mrs. Casa, are* **you** *coming with me?*

> Do you need familiar or formal forms? Formal.
> Is the *you* singular or plural? Plural.
> Then the form is **Loro.**

Signori Casa, **Loro** vengono con me?

- *John, are* **you** *coming with me?*

> Do you need familiar or formal forms? Familiar.
> Is the *you* singular or plural? Singular.
> Then the form is **tu.**

Giovanni, **tu** vieni con me?

- *Mario and Gloria, are* **you** *coming with me?*

> Do you need familiar or formal forms? Familiar.
> Is the *you* singular or plural? Plural.
> Then the form is **voi.**

Mario e Gloria, **voi** venite con me?

What is a Verb Conjugation?

A VERB CONJUGATION is a list of the six possible forms of the verb for a particular tense;[1] there is one verb form for each of the six persons used as the subject of the verb. (See **What is a Subject Pronoun?**, p. 32.)

In English: Most verbs change very little. Let us look at the various forms of the verb *to sing* when each of the possible pronouns is the performer of the action.

1st. per. sing.	*I sing* with the music.
2nd per. sing.	*You sing* with the music.
3rd per. sing.	*He sings* with the music.
	She sings with the music.
	It sings with the music.
1st per. pl.	*We sing* with the music.
2nd per. pl.	*You sing* with the music.
3rd per. pl.	*They sing* with the music.

There is only one change in the verb forms; in the 3rd person singular the verb adds an "-s." Conjugating verbs in English is relatively easy since there are only two forms. This is definitely not the case in Italian.

In Italian: There are six different forms of the verb which correspond to each of the six persons. Memorizing six forms for each verb separately would be an endless task. However, since most verbs follow a regular pattern, only one sample need be memorized. The pattern can then be applied to other verbs of the same group. These are called REGULAR VERBS.

There is a smaller group of verbs whose forms do not follow a regular pattern and must be memorized individually. These are called IRREGULAR VERBS.

---

[1]In this section we shall limit ourselves to the present tense, see p. 52.

A. Subject

Let us now conjugate in Italian the verb *to sing* which we conjugated before in English. Pay special attention to the subject.

lst per. sing.	**io** canto
2nd per. sing.	**tu** canti
3rd per. sing.	{ **lui** canta { **lei** canta { **Lei** canta
lst per. pl.	**noi** cantiamo
2nd per. pl.	**voi** cantate
3rd per. pl.	{ **loro** cantano { **Loro** cantano

Examine the six persons of the verb conjugation and the possible subjects which correspond to each person.

- **1ST PERSON SINGULAR**—The *I form* of the verb (the **io** form) is used whenever the person speaking is the doer of the action.

   Generalmente **io canto** molto bene.
   Normally, I sing very well.

   Notice that **io** is not capitalized except as the first word of a sentence.

- **2ND PERSON SINGULAR**—The *you familiar singular form* of the verb (the **tu** form) is used whenever the person spoken to (with whom you are on familiar terms) is the doer of the action.

   Giovanni, **tu canti** molto bene.
   John, you sing very well.

- **3RD PERSON SINGULAR**—The *3rd person singular form* of the verb (the **lui, lei** form) is used with many possible subjects.

   1. the third person singular masculine pronoun **lui** *(he)* and the third person singular feminine pronoun **lei** *(she)*:

Lui canta molto bene.
He sings very well.

Lei canta molto bene.
She sings very well.

2. The singular pronoun **Lei** (formal *you*):

Signorina Dini, **Lei canta** molto bene.
*Miss Dini, **you sing** very well.*

3. One proper name:

Maria **canta** molto bene.
*Mary **sings** very well.*

4. A singular noun:

Il ragazzo **canta** molto bene.
*The boy **sings** very well.*

L'uccello **canta** molto bene.
*The bird **sings** very well.*

- 1ST PERSON PLURAL—The *we form* of the verb (the **noi** form) is used whenever "I" (the speaker) is one of the doers of the action; that is, whenever the speaker is included in a plural or multiple subject.

  *Isabella, Gloria and I **sing** very well.*
  |
  In Italian: **noi** verb form

  Io, Isabella e Gloria **cantiamo** molto bene.

In the sentence above the subject could be replaced by the pronoun *we*, so that in Italian you must use the **noi** form (1st person plural) of the verb.

- **2ND PERSON PLURAL**—The *you familiar plural form* of the verb (the **voi** form) is used when you are addressing two or more persons with whom you would use **tu** individually.

> *Mary, Susan and you sing very well.*
> In Italian: **voi** verb form

> Tu, Maria e Susanna **cantate** molto bene.

In the sentence above, you say **tu** to each person individually so the subjects could be replaced by the familiar plural *you:* **voi**. In Italian you must use the **voi** (second person plural) form of the verb.

- **3RD PERSON PLURAL**—The *they form* of the verb (the **loro** form) is used with many possible subjects.

1. the third person plural masculine and feminine pronoun **loro** *(they):*

> **Loro cantano** molto bene.
> *They sing very well.*

2. the plural pronoun **Loro** (formal *you*):

> Signori Casa, **Loro cantano** molto bene.
> *Mr. and Mrs. Casa, you sing very well.*

3. two or more proper names:

> *Isabel, Gloria and Robert sing very well.*
> In Italian: **loro** verb form

> Isabella, Gloria e Roberto **cantano** molto bene.

4. two or more singular nouns:

*The girl and her father **sing** very well.*

In Italian: **loro** verb form

La ragazza e suo padre **cantano** molto bene.

5. a plural noun:

*The girls **sing** very well.*

In Italian: **loro** verb form

Le ragazze **cantano** molto bene.

B. Verb form

Let us again look at the conjugation of the same verb *to sing* paying special attention to the verb forms. Notice that each of the six persons has a different verb form. However, when several pronouns belong to the same person there is only one verb form. The 3rd person singular has three pronouns: **lui** *(he)*, **lei** *(she)*, **Lei** *(you)*, but they all have the same verb form: **canta.** The third person plural has two pronouns **loro** *(they)* and **Loro** *(you)*, but one form: **cantano.**

io	cant**o**
tu	cant**i**
lui ⎫ lei ⎬ Lei ⎭	cant**a**
noi	cant**iamo**
voi	cant**ate**
loro ⎫ Loro ⎭	cant**ano**

The Italian verb is composed of two parts:

1. The STEM (also called the ROOT) which is found by dropping the last three letters from the infinitive (see **What is an Infinitive?**, p. 23).

Infinitive	Stem
cant**are**	cant-
tem**ere**	tem-
apr**ire**	apr-

The stem does not change throughout a conjugation.

2. The ENDING which changes for each person in the conjugation of regular and irregular verbs.

Italian verbs are divided into three groups, also called CONJU-GATIONS, based on the infinitive ending. The three endings are:

-are	**-ere**	**-ire**
1st conjugation	2nd conjugation	3rd conjugation

Each of the three verb conjugations has its own set of verb endings. You will have to memorize only one sample verb for each conjugation in order to conjugate any regular verb which belongs to that group. As an example, let's look more closely at regular verbs of the first conjugation, that is, verbs like **cantare** *(to sing),* **parlare** *(to speak),* or **imparare** *(to learn)* which have the same infinitive ending **-are.** Here are the present tense endings (see **What is the Present Tense?**, p. 52):

Subject	Ending
io	-o
tu	-i
lui lei Lei	-a

noi	-iamo
voi	-ate
loro ⎫ Loro ⎭	-ano

After you have memorized the endings for a verb like **cantare,** you can then conjugate any regular **-are** verb. Let's conjugate the verbs **parlare** and **imparare,** in the present tense.

1. Identify the conjugation of the verb by its infinitive endings.

    -are or first conjugation

2. Find the verb stem.

    parl**are** ⟶ parl-   impar**are** ⟶ impar-

3. Add the ending that agrees with the subject.

Subject	Verb form	Verb form
io	parl**o**	impar**o**
tu	parl**i**	impar**i**
lui ⎫ lei ⎬ Lei ⎭	parl**a**	impar**a**
noi	parl**iamo**	impar**iamo**
voi	parl**ate**	impar**ate**
loro ⎫ Loro ⎭	parl**ano**	impar**ano**

The endings for **-ere** and **-ire** verbs will be different, but the process of conjugation is always the same for regular verbs:

1. Identify the conjugation of the verb by its infinitive ending.
2. Find the verb stem.
3. According to the conjugation, add the ending that agrees with the subject.

As you can see, in Italian the verb ending indicates the subject. For instance, **parlo** can only have **io** as a subject. Similarly, the subject of **parli** can only be **tu;** the subject of **parliamo, noi;** the subject of **parlate, voi.** Since you know the subject from the verb form, the subject pronoun is often omitted.

I speak	parlo
you speak	parli
we speak	parliamo
you speak	parlate

If you do include it, the subject pronoun adds strong emphasis to the subject:

io canto

I sing (but he doesn't)

noi cantiamo

we sing (but they don't)

However, in the third person singular and plural it is often necessary to include the pronoun in order to avoid any doubt about who is the subject of the verb.

parla   *could be*   { **lui** parla   *he speaks*
                       lei parla   *she speaks*
                       Lei parla   *you speak*

parlano   *could be*   { **loro** parlano   *they speak*
                         Loro parlano   *you speak*

Note: Subject pronouns are used far less frequently in Italian than in English. You use them only to add emphasis or to clarify the subject.

What are Affirmative and Negative Sentences?

A sentence can be classified as to whether or not it states in a positive way the information it contains. An AFFIRMATIVE SENTENCE states in a positive way the information it contains; it *affirms* the information.

> John works in a factory.
> Italy is a country in Europe.
> They like to travel.

A NEGATIVE SENTENCE does not state in a positive way the information it contains; it *negates* the information.

> John does not work in a shoe store.
> Italy is not a country in Asia.
> They do not like to travel by bus.

In English: An affirmative sentence can become a negative sentence:

• by adding the word ***not*** after the verb.

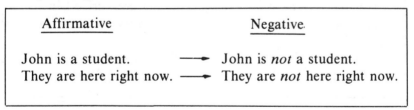

Frequently the word *not* is attached to the verb and the letter "o" is replaced by an apostrophe; this is called a CONTRACTION.

> John *isn't* a student.
> (is not)

> They *aren't* here right now.
> (are not)

- by adding the auxiliary verbs DO/DOES/DID + NOT + THE MAIN VERB IN THE PLAIN INFINITIVE or dictionary form. (See **What is an Infinitive?**, p. 23.)

Affirmative		Negative
We study a lot.	⟶	We *do not study* a lot.
Julia writes well.	⟶	Julia *does not write* well.
The train arrived.	⟶	The train *did not arrive.*

In Italian: The procedure for turning an affirmative sentence into a negative sentence is simpler than in English. You merely place the word **non** in front of the conjugated verb.

Affirmative		Negative
Studiamo molto. *We study a lot.*	⟶	**Non** studiamo molto. *We **do not** study a lot.*
Giulia scrive bene. *Julia writes well.*	⟶	Giulia **non** scrive bene. *Julia **does not** write well.*
Il treno è arrivato. *The train arrived.*	⟶	Il treno **non** è arrivato. *The train **did not** arrive.*

Remember that there is no equivalent for the auxiliary words *do/does/did* in Italian; do not try to include them in a negative sentence.

What are Declarative and Interrogative Sentences?

Sentences are classified according to their purpose. A DECLARATIVE SENTENCE is a sentence that contains a statement.

Columbus discovered America in 1492.

An INTERROGATIVE SENTENCE is a sentence that contains a question.

When did Columbus discover America?

In written language, an interrogative sentence always has a question mark at the end.

In English: A declarative sentence can become an interrogative sentence:

• by adding the helping verb *DO/DOES/DID* BEFORE THE SUBJECT

Statement	Question
Paul and Mary go out together. ⟶	*Do* Paul and Mary go out together?
Mark likes pretty girls. ⟶	*Does* Mark like pretty girls?
Frank and June just got married. ⟶	*Did* Frank and June just get married?

Do/does/did indicates that what follows is a question.

• by inverting the word order from subject + verb to VERB + SUBJECT

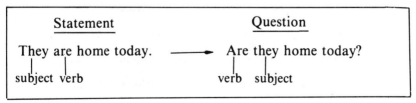

Statement	Question
They are home today. ⟶	Are they home today?
subject verb	verb subject

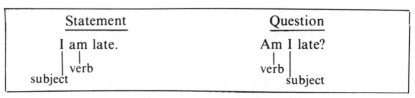

This reversing of the normal "subject + verb" order is called INVERSION.

In Italian: A declarative sentence can become an interrogative sentence by placing the subject after the verb; the word order of the question is VERB + SUBJECT.

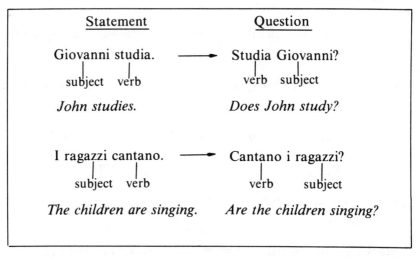

Note: Be sure to ignore the auxiliary verb *does/do/did* when using Italian. Italian has no such helping verbs.

When a statement consists of a subject and verb plus one or two words, those few words are usually placed between them. The word order of the question is VERB + REMAINDER + SUBJECT.

Statement	Question
Giovanni studia inglese.⟶	Studia inglese Giovanni?
subject verb remainder	verb remainder subject
John studies English.	*Does John study English?*

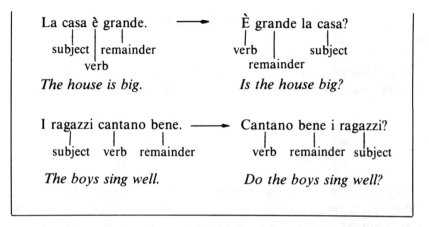

In English and in Italian you can also transform a statement into a question by adding a short phrase at the end of the statement. This short phrase is called a TAG or TAG QUESTION.

In English: The tag question repeats the idea of the statement in a negative way.

> John is a nice guy, *isn't he?*
> We study a lot, *don't we?*

The end part of the statement *(isn't he, don't we)* is the tag or tag question.

In Italian: The words **no?, vero?** or **non è vero?** can be added to a statement to form a tag question.

> Giovanni è un bravo ragazzo, **no?**
> *John is a nice guy, **isn't he?***
>
> Lavori molto, **vero?**
> *You work hard, **don't you?***
>
> Oggi è mercoledì, **non è vero?**
> *Today is Wednesday, **isn't it?***

What is Meant by Tense?

The TENSE of a verb indicates the time when the action of the verb takes place (at the present time, in the past, or in the future).

I am eating.	Present
I ate.	Past
I will eat.	Future

As you can see in the above examples, just by putting the verb in a different tense and without giving any additional information (such as "I am eating *now*," "I ate *yesterday*," "I will eat *tomorrow*"), you can indicate when the action of the verb takes place.

Tenses may be classified according to the way they are formed. A SIMPLE TENSE consists of only one verb form and a COMPOUND TENSE consists of two or more verb forms.

In English: There are only two simple tenses: the present and the past.

> I study
> I studied

All of the others are compound tenses, formed by one or more auxiliary verbs plus the main verb.

> I have studied
> I will study
> I would study
> I will have studied

In Italian: There are more simple tenses than in English.

studio	*I study*	Present
studiai	*I studied*	Simple past
studiavo	*I was studying*	Imperfect
studierò	*I will study*	Future
studierei	*I would study*	Conditional

As in the last three examples, there is frequently a lack of correspondence between Italian and English. English has compound tenses where Italian uses simple tenses, since the meaning of *was, will, would* is contained in the verb endings.

There are compound tenses in Italian. They are formed by the auxiliary verbs **avere** and **essere** plus the past participle of the main verb.

ho studiato	*I have studied*	Present perfect
avevo studiato	*I had studied*	Past perfect
avrò studiato	*I will have studied*	Future perfect

This handbook discusses these tenses in separate sections.

What is the Present Tense?

The PRESENT TENSE indicates that the action is going on at the present time. It can be:

- at the time the speaker is speaking

    I *see* you.

- a habitual action

    He *smokes* when he *is* nervous.

- a general truth

    The sun *shines* every day.

In English: There are three forms of the verb which, although they have a slightly different meaning, all indicate the present tense.

Mary *studies* in the library.	<u>Present</u>
Mary *is studying* in the library.	<u>Present progressive</u>
Mary *does study* in the library.	<u>Present emphatic</u>

In Italian: The SIMPLE PRESENT TENSE is used to express the meanings of the present, present progressive and present emphatic tenses in English. In Italian the idea of present tense is indicated by the ending of the verb, without any auxiliary verb such as *is* and *does*. It is very important, therefore, not to translate these auxiliary verbs used in English. Simply put the main verb in the present tense.

*Mary **studies** in the library.*

studia

*Mary **is studying** in the library.*

studia

Mary ⌐does study⌐ in the library.

studia

There is a present progressive tense in Italian, but since it is not used in the same manner as the English present progressive, we have discussed it in a separate section. (See **What is a Progressive Tense?**, p. 56.)

What are the Special Uses of the Verbs *Avere* **(to have) and** *Essere* **(to be)?**

The verbs *to have* and *to be* are irregular verbs in Italian whose conjugation has to be memorized. They are important verbs because they serve both as main verbs and auxiliary verbs.

• main verb

Maria **ha** tre sorelle.
*Mary **has** three sisters.*

Paolo **è** italiano.
*Paul **is** Italian.*

• auxiliary verb

Maria **ha visto** Carlo.
*Mary **has seen** Charles.*

Paolo **è uscito.**
*Paul **has gone out.***

The use of **avere** and **essere** as auxiliaries is discussed in detail on p. 68.

The use of **avere** and **essere** as main verbs is somewhat different in Italian from the use of *to have* and *to be* in English. Some of these are idiomatic expressions (see p. 2) and are not easily translatable from one language to another. Here are a few examples:

1. Many English expressions using the verb *to be* are translated with the verb **avere** *(to have)* in Italian.

- **Ho** sete.
  to have

  I am thirsty.
  to be

- **Ho** venti anni.
  to have

  I am twenty years old.
  to be

- **Hai** sonno?
  to have

  Are you sleepy?
  to be

2. The English expressions *there is* and *there are* are translated in two different ways depending on their meaning.

- c'è *(there is)* | ci sono *(there are)*—to describe, explain or give the location of something or someone.

   C'è una farmacia in centro.
   There is a drugstore downtown.

   Ci sono molti ragazzi per strada.
   There are many boys on the street.

- ecco *(there is* or *there are)*—to point out something or someone.

   Ecco il libro.
   There is the book.

   Ecco i miei amici.
   There are my friends.

Notice that **ecco** is invariable (it does not change) and that it is not followed by a verb.

Do not confuse **c'è, ci sono** with **ecco. Ecco** is "to point out" and **c'è/ci sono** are "to describe."

   C'è un nuovo professore d'italiano.
   There is a new Italian professor. [at our school]

   Ecco il nuovo professore d'italiano.
   There is the new Italian professor. [pointing him out]

What is a Progressive Tense?

The PROGRESSIVE TENSES are used to emphasize that an action is in progress at a certain moment.

John *is talking* on the phone.   (Now.)
We *were trying* to start the car.   (At that moment.)

In English: The progressive tenses are made up of the auxiliary verb *TO BE* + THE PRESENT PARTICIPLE OF THE MAIN VERB. The present participle is the *-ing* form of the verb (see p. 59): *talking, trying, leaving, washing.*

    We *are leaving* right now.

       | present| participle
present| tense
of *to be*

    At that moment John *was washing* his car.

         | present| participle
       past tense
       of *to be*

Notice that it is the tense of the auxiliary verb *to be* which indicates when the action of the main verb takes place.

In Italian: The progressive tenses are made up of the auxiliary verb *STARE* + THE *GERUNDIO* OF THE MAIN VERB. The **gerundio**[1] form of the verb must be used while English uses the *-ing* form. The **gerundio** is formed by adding **-ando** to the stem of **-are** verbs and **-endo** to the stem of **-ere** and **-ire** verbs.

---

[1]Do not confuse the term **gerundio** which is an Italian verb form with *gerund* which is a verbal noun (see pp. 61-64).

Infinitive	Stem	Gerundio
cant**are**	cant-	cant**ando**
tem**ere**	tem-	tem**endo**
part**ire**	part-	part**endo**

A progressive form of the verb exists for all the tenses in Italian. However, we shall here be concerned only with the present progressive. The **PRESENT PROGRESSIVE** is made up of the PRESENT TENSE OF *STARE* + *GERUNDIO* OF THE MAIN VERB.

• **Stiamo uscendo** in questo stesso momento.

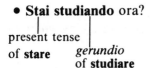

present tense
of **stare**   *gerundio*
          of **uscire**

We are going out at this very moment.

• **Stai studiando** ora?

present tense
of **stare**   *gerundio*
          of **studiare**

Are you studying right now?

The progressive tenses are used far more frequently in English than in Italian. Make sure that in Italian you use them only when you want to emphasize that an action is happening at a particular moment.

Compare the use of the present tense and present progressive tense in the sentences below.

• *John, what are you studying in school?*

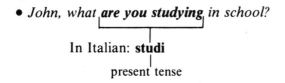

In Italian: **studi**

present tense

58

The present tense is used because you are asking what John is studying in general.

John, what **are you studying** *now?*

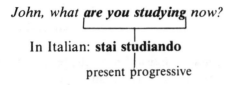

In Italian: **stai studiando**

present progressive

The present progressive is used because the word *now* indicates that you want to know what John is studying at this particular time as opposed to all other times.

• *Mary,* **are you working** *for the government?*

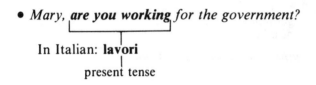

In Italian: **lavori**

present tense

The present tense is used because you are asking where Mary is working in general.

Mary, **are you working** *right now?*

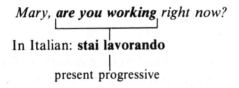

In Italian: **stai lavorando**

present progressive

The present progressive is used because the words *right now* indicate that you want to know if Mary is working at this particular time as opposed to all other times.

Note: Do not use the present progressive to state general truths or habitual action; use the present tense instead. (See **What is the Present Tense?**, p. 52.)

What is a Participle?

A PARTICIPLE has two functions: 1. It is a form of the verb that is used in combination with an auxiliary verb to indicate certain tenses. 2. It may be used as an adjective or modifier to describe something.

I *was* ***writing*** a letter.
auxiliary
      participle

The *broken* vase was on the floor.
    participle describing *vase*

There are two types of participles: the PRESENT PARTICIPLE and the PAST PARTICIPLE. As you will learn in your study of Italian, participles are not used in the same way in the two languages.

A. The present participle

In English: The present participle is easy to recognize because it is the **-ing** form of the verb: *working, studying, dancing, playing.*

The present participle is used:

• as an adjective

This is an *amazing* discovery.
   describes the noun *discovery*

She read an *interesting* book.
   describes the noun *book*

● in a verbal function

1. as the main verb in progressive tenses (see p. 56)

She is *singing*.
└─────┬─────┘

present progressive of *to sing*

They were *dancing*.
└──────┬──────┘

past progressive of *to dance*

2. in a participial phrase

(By) *studying* hard, Tony learned Italian.
└──────────┬──────────┘

participial phrase

I burned myself (while) *cooking*.
└────────┬────────┘

participial phrase

Prepositions such as *by, while, on,* and *in* are often found in participial phrases, but they can be left out.

In Italian: The present participle is formed by adding **-ante** to the stem of **-are** and **-ente** to the stem of **-ere** and **-ire** verbs.

Infinitive	Stem	Present participle
interess**are**	interess-	interess**ante**
sorprend**ere**	sorprend-	sorprend**ente**
segu**ire**	segu-	segu**ente**

The only use of the present participle which is similar to English is its use as an adjective.

Questa è una scoperta **sorprendente**.
*This is an **amazing** discovery.*

Ha letto un libro **interessante.**
*She read an **interesting** book.*

Otherwise, the present participle is not used in the same way in Italian as in English. The verbal functions of the English present participle are expressed in Italian by the **gerundio** (see p. 56).

1. The progressive tenses are made up of the auxiliary verb STARE+ THE GERUNDIO OF THE MAIN VERB. See **What is a Progressive Tense?**, p. 56 for a detailed study.

present progressive

• *She is **singing.***

present participle

Sta **cantando.**

present   gerundio

stare   **cantare**

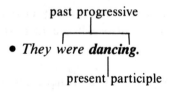

past progressive

• *They were **dancing.***

present participle

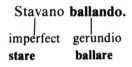

Stavano **ballando.**

imperfect   gerundio

stare   **ballare**

2. The participial phrase is expressed with the **gerundio.**

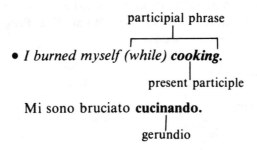

participial phrase

• *(By) **studying** hard, Tony learned Italian.*

present participle

Studiando sodo, Tony ha imparato l'italiano.

gerundio

participial phrase

• *I burned myself (while) **cooking.***

present participle

Mi sono bruciato **cucinando.**

gerundio

Notice that prepositions *(by, while)* have no equivalents in the Italian participial phrase.

An English verb ending in *-ing* is not always a present participle; it can be a verbal noun. A VERBAL NOUN, also called a GERUND,[1] is a noun which is formed from a verb.

In English: The verbal noun ends in *-ing* and can function in almost any way a noun can. It can be the subject, direct object, indirect object and an object of a preposition.

Reading can be fun.

noun subject

Mario prefers *reading.*

noun object

---

[1]Do not confuse the term *gerund* which is an English verbal noun with **gerundio** which is an Italian verb form.

Before *leaving,* call me.

noun object of preposition

In Italian: The English gerund is expressed with the infinitive of the verb.

- **Leggere** è divertente.

infinitive

Reading is fun.

gerund

- Mario preferisce **leggere.**

infinitive

Mario prefers reading.

gerund

- Prima di **partire,** telefonami.

infinitive

Before leaving, call me.

gerund

For reference, here is a chart identifying the various English *-ing* forms and their Italian equivalents.

English -*ing*	Italian
Adjective	
present participle ⟶	present participle
ex. the *reading* public	$\begin{cases} \text{-are} \longrightarrow \text{-ante} \\ \text{-ere/-ire} \longrightarrow \text{-ente} \end{cases}$
Verb	
Progressive tenses:	
to be + present participle ⟶	various simple tenses
ex. What are you *reading?*	present
What were you *reading?*	past
etc.	etc.
to be + present participle ⟶	**stare** + gerundio
ex. What are you *reading* now?	$\begin{cases} \text{-are} \longrightarrow \text{-ando} \\ \text{-ere/-ire} \longrightarrow \text{-endo} \end{cases}$
Participial phrase:	
present participle ⟶	gerundio
ex. (while) *reading*	
Noun	
gerund ⟶	infinitive
ex. *Reading* is fun.	**-are/ -ere/ -ire**

B. The past participle

In English: The past participle is formed in several ways. You can always find it by remembering the form of the verb you would use following *I have: I have* **spoken,** *I have* **written,** *I have* **walked.**

The past participle is used:

• as an adjective

Is the *written* word more important
than the *spoken* word?

Written describes the noun word.
Spoken describes the noun word.

• as a verb form in combination with the auxiliary verb *have*

I have *written* all that I have to say.
He hasn't *spoken* to me since our quarrel.

In Italian: A verb can have a regular past participle, that is, a past
participle formed according to the regular pattern: **-are** verbs add
-ato to the stem; **-ere** verbs add **-uto,** and **-ire** verbs add **-ito.**

Infinitive	Stem	Past participle
cant**are**	cant-	cant**ato**
tem**ere**	tem-	tem**uto**
part**ire**	part-	part**ito**

You will have to memorize irregular past participles individually.
As you can see in the three examples below they are very different
from the infinitive.

Infinitive	Stem	Past participle
mettere	mett-	messo
scrivere	scriv-	scritto
leggere	legg-	letto

As in English, the past participle can be used as an adjective or as a
verb form.

- When the past participle is used as an adjective it must agree with the noun it modifies in gender and in number.

  *the **spoken** language*

  > *Spoken* modifies the noun *language*.
  > Since the Italian word for *language* is feminine singular **(la lingua)**, the word for *spoken* must also be feminine singular.

  la lingua **parlata**

  *the **broken** records*

  > *Broken* modifies the noun *records*.
  > Since the Italian word for *records* is masculine plural **(i dischi)**, the word for *broken* must also be masculine plural.

  i dischi **rotti**

- The most important use of the past participle in Italian is as a verb form in combination with the auxiliary verbs **avere** and **essere** to form the "perfect" tenses. (See **What is the Past Tense?**, p. 67.)

What is the Past Tense?

The PAST TENSE is used to express an action that occurred in the past.

In English: There are several verb forms that indicate that the action took place in the past.

I worked	Simple past
I was working	Past progressive
I used to work	With helping verb *used to*
I did work	Past emphatic
I have worked	Present perfect

In Italian: There are many verb tenses which can be used to express an action which occurred in the past. Each tense has its own set of endings and its own rules which tell us when and how to use it. We will here be concerned with only two of the past tenses in Italian: the imperfect **(l'imperfetto)** and the present perfect **(il passato prossimo).**

The IMPERFECT is formed by adding certain endings to the stem of the verb. Its conjugation is quite regular so that there is no need to add to what is in your Italian textbook on how to form the tense.

The PRESENT PERFECT is composed of the PRESENT TENSE OF the auxiliary verbs *AVERE* OR *ESSERE* + THE PAST PARTICIPLE.

According to the auxiliary verb used **(avere** or **essere,** see below), the past participle follows certain rules of agreement which your Italian grammar book outlines. Since the past participle conjugated with **essere** agrees with the subject, go over the section **What is a Subject?**, p. 28. Past participles conjugated with **avere** agree with the direct object if it comes before the verb. You should go over the section **What are Objects?**, p. 138.

A. Avere or Essere

Unlike English where the past participle is used with the verb *to have* (see p. 64), the past participle in Italian can be used with either **avere** or **essere**.

ho mangiato
|
present |
avere past participle
mangiare

I have eaten

sono andato
|
present |
essere past participle
andare

I have gone

Your problem will be determining whether a verb takes **avere** or **essere**. As a rule, transitive verbs (the verbs which can take a direct object) are conjugated with **avere**. The intransitive verbs (the verbs which cannot take a direct object) are generally conjugated with **essere**. These are very broad rules and there are many exceptions. When you are in doubt about which auxiliary to use, consult an Italian dictionary under the verb infinitive.

Transitive — *avere*

- I { *have eaten* / *ate* } an apple.
    direct object

Ho mangiato una mela.

- *The students* $\begin{cases} \textbf{\textit{have learned}} \\ \textbf{\textit{learned}} \end{cases}$ *the lesson.*

                                direct object

Gli studenti **hanno imparato** la lezione.

Intransitive — *essere*

- *Mary* $\begin{cases} \textbf{\textit{has gone}} \\ \textbf{\textit{went}} \end{cases}$ *to the movies.*

Maria **è andata** al cinema.

- *The students* $\begin{cases} \textbf{\textit{have left.}} \\ \textbf{\textit{left.}} \end{cases}$

Gli studenti **sono partiti.**

Note: When the past participle is conjugated with **essere** it must agree in gender and number with the subject of the sentence: **Maria** è andat**a** *(fem. sing.);* **Gli studenti** sono partit**i** *(masc. pl.).*

B. Imperfect or Present perfect

In choosing the correct tense in Italian between the imperfect and the present perfect, the English verb form will rarely tell you in which tense the Italian verb should be. To select the right tense you will have to rely on the rules in your Italian grammar book.

A practical guide to choosing the proper tense is to ask the question "What happened?" The answer will require a verb in the present perfect. The answer to the question "What was going on?" will require a verb in the imperfect.

         I *was reading* when he *came* in.

           imperfect   present perfect

When you ask "What was going on?" the answer is "I was reading" (imperfect). To the question "What happened?" the answer is "he came in" (present perfect). You might also note that there are some English verb forms that indicate when the imperfect should be used.

- If the English verb form includes, or could include, the helping verb *used to* which indicates an habitual or repeated action.

    *On Sundays **I sang** in the choir.*

    I sang may be replaced by *I used to sing;*
    therefore, in Italian, you use the imperfect.

    La domenica **cantavo** nel coro.

- If the English verb form is in the past progressive tense, as *was laughing, were laughing.*

    *He **was** always **laughing**.*
    Rideva sempre.

- Often the verb *was/were* plus an adjective, indicating a past condition (physical, mental or emotional), will require the use of the imperfect in Italian.

    ***She was** sad.*
    Era triste.

    ***They were** rich.*
    Erano ricchi.

You should practice choosing the correct Italian past tense with English texts, without translating them. Pick out the verbs in the past tense and indicate for each one if you would put it in the imperfect or in the present perfect. Remember that selecting one of these two possible past tenses gives the verb a slightly different meaning. Sometimes both tenses are possible, but the meaning of the sentence changes.

1. *He invited Maria to dinner.* (yesterday)
   Ha invitato Maria a cena.

2. *He invited Maria to dinner.* (every day)
   Invitava Maria a cena.

As you see from these examples, the English verb *invited* does not indicate which of the two Italian past tenses is needed. Here, the present perfect indicates that an action took place once (sentence 1). The imperfect emphasizes the repetition of an action (sentence 2).

Note: In your Italian textbook you will find reference to the SIMPLE PAST, also called the PAST ABSOLUTE **(passato remoto)** tense, which is used in literary language instead of the present perfect. You do not need to be concerned with the past absolute for spoken Italian. However, you will need to recognize it for written Italian (short stories, novels, poetry, etc.).

What is the Past Perfect?

The PAST PERFECT tense is used to express an action completed in the past before some other past action or event.

In English: The past perfect is formed with the auxiliary *HAD* (which is the past tense of the verb *to have)* + THE PAST PARTICIPLE.

The past perfect is used when two actions happened at different times in the past and you want to make it clear which of the actions preceded the other.

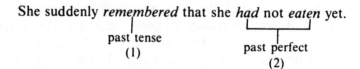

She suddenly *remembered* that she *had* not *eaten* yet.
past tense
(1)
past perfect
(2)

Both action (1) and action (2) occurred in the past, but action (2) preceded action (1). Therefore, action (2) is in the past perfect.

Don't forget that the tense of a verb indicates the time when an action occurred. Therefore, when two verbs in a sentence are in the same tense, we know that the actions took place at the same time. In order to show that they took place at different times, different tenses must be used. Look at the following examples:

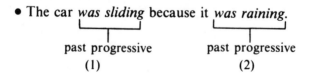

• The car *was sliding* because it *was raining*.
past progressive
(1)
past progressive
(2)

Action (1) and action (2) took place at the same time.

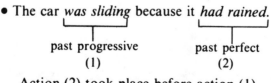

• The car *was sliding* because it *had rained*.
past progressive
(1)
past perfect
(2)

Action (2) took place before action (1).

In Italian: The past perfect, called the **trapassato prossimo,** is formed by the IMPERFECT OF the auxiliary verb *AVERE* OR *ESSERE* + THE PAST PARTICIPLE. The rules of agreement of the past participle are the same as for the present perfect (see p. 67).

The past perfect is used to indicate that an action in the past took place before another action in the past, expressed by the present perfect or the imperfect.

Look at this line showing the relationship of tenses.

Verb tense:	Past perfect	Present perfect	Present	Future
		Imperfect		
Time action takes place:	D	C	A	B
	before "C"	before "A"	now	after "A"

If you look again at the above examples, you will see that in Italian the tense usage is the same as in English. That is, time relationships are expressed in the same way in both languages.

- *The car **was sliding** because it **was raining.***
  La macchina **sbandava** perché **pioveva.**
        imperfect   imperfect
          "C"   "C"

When both verbs are in the imperfect the two actions took place at the same time in the past.

- *The car **was sliding** because it **had rained.***
La macchina **sbandava** perché **aveva piovuto.**

$$\text{sbandava} \rightarrow \text{imperfect "C"} \qquad \text{aveva piovuto} \rightarrow \text{past perfect "D"}$$

The action in the past perfect (point "D") occurred before the action in the imperfect (point "C").

You cannot always rely on English to determine when to use the past perfect. English usage permits the use of the simple past in many cases to describe an action that preceded another, if it is clear which action came first.

*The teacher **wanted** to know who **saw** the student.*

simple past   simple past

*The teacher **wanted** to know who **had seen** the student.*

simple past   past perfect

Although the two sentences above mean the same thing and are correct English, only the verb sequence of the second sentence would be correct in Italian.

Il professore **voleva** sapere chi **aveva veduto** lo studente.

imperfect "C"   past perfect "D"

The verb in the past perfect (point "D") stresses that the action was completed before the action of "wanting to know" (point "C"). In Italian grammar, agreement of tenses is stricter than in English.

What is the Future Tense?

The FUTURE TENSE indicates that an action will take place in the future.

In English: The future tense is a compound tense. It is formed by means of the auxiliary *WILL* OR *SHALL* + THE MAIN VERB.

> Paul and Mary *will do* their work tomorrow.
> I *shall go* out tonight.

In conversation, *shall* and *will* are often shortened to *'ll:* They *'ll do* it tomorrow, I *'ll go* out tonight.

In Italian: You do not need an auxiliary verb to show that the action will take place in the future. Future time is indicated by a simple tense. It is formed with a STEM DERIVED FROM THE INFINITIVE + FUTURE ENDINGS.

- **-are** verbs change to **-er** + future endings

Infinitive	Stem +	Future ending	
parl**are**	parler-	parler**ò**	*I shall speak*
cant**are**	canter-	canter**à**	*she will sing*

- **-ere** and **-ire** verbs drop the final "e" + future endings

Infinitive	Stem +	Future ending	
tem**ere**	temer-	temer**ò**	*I shall fear*
part**ire**	partir-	partir**à**	*he will leave*

- irregular future verb stems + future endings

Infinitive	Stem	+	Future ending	
avere	avr-		avrò	*I shall have*
volere	vorr-		vorrà	*she will want*

Your textbook will indicate which verbs have irregular stems in the future. Be sure to memorize them as the same stem serves to form the conditional (see **What is the Conditional?**, p. 92).

Italian is much stricter than English in its use of tenses. While English uses the present tense after expressions such as *as soon as, when, by the time*, etc. which introduce an action to take place in the future, Italian uses the future.

- Appena **ritornerà,** telefonerò.
  future

*As soon as he **returns**, I will call.*
  present

- Verrà, quando **sarà** pronta.
  future

*She will come when she **is** ready.*
  present

In English and in Italian it is possible to express a future action without using the future tense.

In English: You can use:

- the present progressive of the main verb

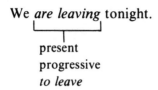

We *are leaving* tonight.

present
progressive
to leave

- the present progressive of *to go* + the infinitive of the main verb

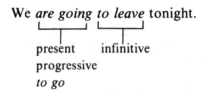

We *are going to leave* tonight.

present   infinitive
progressive
to go

Both of these constructions mean the same as

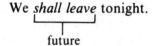

We *shall leave* tonight.

future

In Italian: The above progressive constructions are not used. In the spoken language the present tense commonly replaces the future tense to indicate an action about to take place.

Partiamo stasera.

present

We **shall leave** *tonight.*

future

● Elena **resta** a casa stasera.

    present

*Helen **will stay** home tonight.*

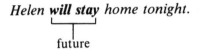

    future

FUTURE OF PROBABILITY—In addition to expressing an action which will take place in the future, in Italian the future tense can be used to express a probable fact: what the speaker feels is probably true. This is called the future of probability.

In English: The idea of probability is expressed with words such as *must, probably, wonder.*

> My keys *must* be around here.
> My keys are *probably* around here.
> I *wonder* if my keys are around here.

In Italian: It is not necessary to use the words *must, probably,* or *wonder* to express probable facts; the main verb is simply put in the future tense.

● Chi **sarà** alla porta?

    main verb
    future tense

*I wonder who **is** at the door.*

    main verb
    present tense

● **Sarà** mia madre.

main verb
future tense

It's probably my mother.

is main verb
present tense

- Non posso trovare il mio libro. **L'avrà** Carlo.

  main verb
  future tense

*I can't find my book. Charles must **have** it.*

  main verb
  present tense

What is the Future Perfect?

The FUTURE PERFECT tense is used to express an action which will be completed in the future before some other future action or by a specific time.

In English: The future perfect is formed with the auxiliaries *WILL HAVE* OR *SHALL HAVE* + THE PAST PARTICIPLE OF THE MAIN VERB: *I shall have taken, he will have gone.*

You will often find the future perfect after the expression *by,* and *by the time.*

- By the time school opens, I shall have finished.

  future action   future perfect
  (1)   (2)

Although the verb tense of action (1) is the present, it refers to a future action (see p. 76). Action (2) is in the future perfect because it will be completed in the future before action (1).

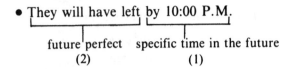

- They will have left by 10:00 P.M.

future perfect   specific time in the future
(2)   (1)

Action (2) is in the future perfect because it will be completed in the future before a specific time in the future (1).

In Italian: The future perfect, called the **futuro anteriore,** is formed by using the auxiliary *AVERE* OR *ESSERE* IN THE FUTURE TENSE + THE PAST PARTICIPLE OF THE MAIN VERB: **avrò preso** *(I shall have taken),* **sarà partito** *(he will have gone).*

When you observe the following line showing the relationship of future tenses, you will see that the future perfect is used in the same way in both languages, but that the future (point "C") is expressed by the present in English and by the future in Italian (see **What is the Future Tense?, p. 75**).

Verb tense:	Present	Future perfect	Present (English) Future (Italian)
	A	B	C
Time action takes place:	now	after "A" and before "C"	after "A"

To use "B" (the future perfect) you have to have an action or event at point "C" with which to contrast it. You do not need "A" in the same sentence.

In the following example, notice that actions taking place at point "B" are in the future perfect tense in both languages, but that actions at point "C" are in the present tense in English and in the future tense in Italian.

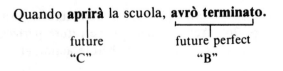

Quando **aprirà** la scuola, **avrò terminato.**

future   future perfect
"C"   "B"

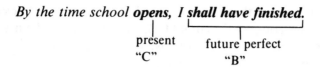

*By the time school **opens,** I **shall have finished.***

present	future perfect
"C"	"B"

Even if there is no action specified at point "C," only a specific time in the future, actions taking place at point "B" are in the future perfect in both languages.

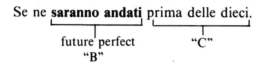

Se ne **saranno andati** prima delle dieci.

future perfect	"C"
"B"	

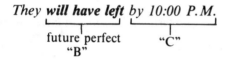

*They **will have left** by 10:00 P.M.*

future perfect	"C"
"B"	

In the following two sentences, the sequence of actions is the same. Compare how the future tense is used to list a series of actions to take place in the future (sentence 1) and how the future perfect is used to stress that a future action will be completed before another (sentence 2).

1. All the verbs are in the future tense (point "C") because you are listing a series of things which will occur in the future, "this evening."

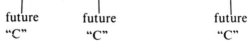

Stasera i bambini **mangeranno** e **andranno** a letto, e poi **usciremo.**

future	future	future
"C"	"C"	"C"

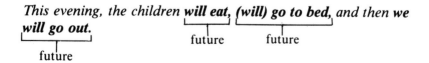

*This evening, the children **will eat,** (will) **go to bed,** and then **we will go out.***

future	future	future

2. In order to stress the actions that will be accomplished before the action of "going out" (point "C"), Italian requires the use of the future perfect (point "B"). English is much less strict in its use of tenses and uses the present perfect.

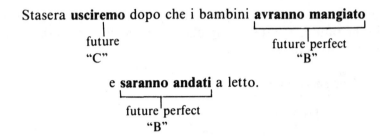

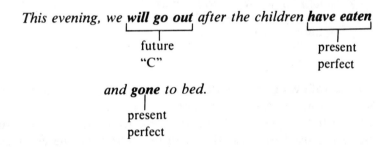

When encountering sentences which refer to future actions, be sure to establish the sequence of events which will enable you to select the tense required in Italian.

What is Meant by Mood?

The many forms a verb can take are divided into different moods. The word mood is a variation of the word *mode* meaning manner or way. The mood is the form of the verb which indicates the attitude (mode) of the speaker toward what he is saying. As a beginning student of Italian, all you have to know are the names of the moods so that you will understand what your Italian textbook is referring to. You will learn when to use the various moods as you learn verbs and their tenses.

In English: Verbs can be in one of three moods:

1. The INDICATIVE MOOD is used to express or indicate facts. This is the most common mood and most verb forms that you use in everyday conversation belong to the indicative mood.

>   Robert *studies* Italian.
>   Mary *is* here.

The present tense (see p. 52), the past tense (see p. 67), and the future tense (see p. 75) are all examples of tenses in the indicative mood.

2. The IMPERATIVE MOOD is used to express a command (see p. 84).

>   Robert, *study* Italian now!
>   Mary, *be* here on time!

3. The SUBJUNCTIVE MOOD is used to express a potential fact; it stresses the speaker's feelings about the fact and is "subjective" about those facts.

>   The professor insists that Robert *study* Italian.
>   I wish that Mary *were* here.

In Italian: The Italian language identifies four moods, instead of the English three. In addition to the three moods listed above, there is the CONDITIONAL MOOD (see p. 92). As in English, the indicative mood is the most common mood and most of the tenses you will learn belong to the indicative mood.

What is the Imperative?

The IMPERATIVE is the command form of a verb. It is used to give someone an order.

In English: There are two types of commands.

1. The YOU COMMAND is used when giving an order to one person or many persons. The dictionary form of the verb is used for the *you* command.

Affirmative	Negative
Answer the phone.	Don't *answer* the phone.
Clean your room.	Don't *clean* your room.
Talk softly.	Don't *talk* softly.

Notice that the pronoun "you" is not stated. The absence of the pronoun *you* in the sentence is a good indication that you are dealing with an imperative and not a present tense. Compare the following sentences:

Present tense (statement)	Imperative (affirmative command)	Imperative (negative command)
You answer the phone.	*Answer* the phone.	*Don't answer* the phone.
You clean your room.	*Clean* your room.	*Don't clean* your room.
You talk softly.	*Talk* softly.	*Don't talk* softly.

2. The *WE* COMMAND is used when the speaker gives an order to himself as well as to others. In English this command begins with the phrase "let's" followed by the dictionary form of the verb.

Let's leave.   *Let's not leave.*
Let's go to the movies.   *Let's not go* to the movies.

In Italian: Italian uses the same two basic types of commands: the *YOU* COMMAND and the *WE* COMMAND.

1. *YOU* COMMAND

The form you use depends on two factors:

Which form of "you" is appropriate in Italian: **tu, voi, Lei, Loro.** (See **What is Meant by Familiar and Formal You?**, p. 34.)

If you need a familiar *you* **(tu, voi)** you will also have to determine if it is an affirmative command (an order to do something) or a negative command (an order not to do something).

It is only after you have answered the above questions that you will be ready to select the correct command form in Italian.

Here are examples of each form:

- The **tu** command (familiar singular *you*) is used to give an order to a person you know well, a child or an animal.

The affirmative **tu** command has the following forms:

-are verbs—the 3rd person singular of the present

Parla!	*Speak!*
Guarda!	*Look!*

-ere, -ire verbs—the 2nd person singular of the present

Scrivi!	*Write!*
Senti!	*Listen!*

There are a few irregular forms which you will have to learn individually.

The negative **tu** command of all verbs is the same as the infinitive.

Non parlare!	*Don't speak!*
Non scrivere!	*Don't write!*
Non sentire!	*Don't listen!*

- The **voi** command (familiar plural *you*) is used to give an order to two or more persons you know well, children, or animals. The affirmative and the negative **voi** commands have the same form as the 2nd person plural of the present indicative.

Affirmative		Negative	
Parlate!	*Speak!*	Non parlate!	*Don't speak!*
Scrivete!	*Write!*	Non scrivete!	*Don't write!*
Sentite!	*Listen!*	Non sentite!	*Don't listen!*

- The **Lei** command (formal singular *you*) is used to give an order to a person you do not know well, or a person you view with respect. The affirmative and negative **Lei** commands have the same form as the 3rd person singular of the present subjunctive.

Affirmative		Negative	
Parli!	*Speak!*	Non parli!	*Don't speak!*
Scriva!	*Write!*	Non scriva!	*Don't write!*
Senta!	*Listen!*	Non senta!	*Don't listen!*

- The **Loro** command (formal plural *you*) is used to give an order to two or more persons you don't know well, or persons you view with respect. The affirmative and negative **Loro** commands have the same form as the 3rd person plural of the present subjunctive.

Affirmative		Negative	
Parlino!	*Speak!*	Non parlino!	*Don't speak!*
Scrivano!	*Write!*	Non scrivano!	*Don't write!*
Sentano!	*Listen!*	Non sentano!	*Don't listen!*

The use of the pronoun **Lei** or **Loro** following the command is optional. It is considered somewhat more polite to use the pronoun, but it is not rude to omit it.

2. *WE* COMMAND

The affirmative and negative **noi** command has the same form as the first person plural of the present indicative.

Affirmative		Negative	
Parliamo!	*Let's speak!*	Non parliamo!	*Let's not speak!*
Scriviamo!	*Let's write!*	Non scriviamo!	*Let's not write!*
Sentiamo!	*Let's listen!*	Non sentiamo!	*Let's not listen!*

Notice that the English phrase *let's* is not translated in Italian; the command ending is the equivalent of *let's*.

Here is a chart you can use as a reference:

Command Form	Affirmative	Negative
tu	Present indicative **-are:** 3rd pers. sing. **-ere, -ire:** 2nd pers. sing.	Infinitive
voi	Present indicative 2nd pers. pl.	Present indicative 2nd pers. pl.
Lei	Present subjunctive 3rd pers. sing.	Present subjunctive 3rd pers. sing.
Loro	Present subjunctive 3rd pers. pl.	Present subjunctive 3rd pers. pl.
noi	Present indicative 1st pers. pl.	Present indicative 1st pers. pl.

Note: All of the imperative forms, except the **tu** forms, are the same in the affirmative and negative.

What is the Subjunctive?

The SUBJUNCTIVE is the mood of the verb which is used to express actions that are unreal, actions that are not actual fact. Notice the difference between the indicative mood (used to express facts) and the subjunctive mood in the following examples:

Indicative

- States a fact

  John *is* here.

- States something that can be a fact

  If John *is* here, you can meet him.

  Implication: There is the possibility that John is here.

Subjunctive

- States something that is contrary-to-fact

  If John *were* here, you could meet him.

  Implication: John is not here, and you cannot meet him.

  I wish John *were* here.

  Implication: But he is not.

In English: The subjunctive is difficult to recognize because it resembles the indicative. But the subjunctive does exist and you often use it without realizing it. Because the subjunctive is most readily recognizable in the verb *to be*, we will use the verb *to be* to illustrate the difference between the indicative and the subjunctive in the sentences below:

- I *am* in Europe right now.
  |
  indicative

  I wish I *were* in Europe right now.
  |
  subjunctive

- Mary *is* intelligent.
  |
  indicative

  If Mary *were* intelligent, she would learn faster.
  |
  subjunctive

The subjunctive occurs most commonly in three kinds of sentences:

1. Conditions contrary-to-fact, usually using *if,* the "*if*-condition clause." (See **What is the Conditional?**, p. 92.)

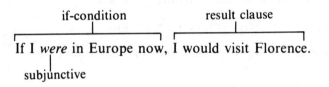

     if-condition   result clause

If I *were* in Europe now, I would visit Florence.
  |
subjunctive

     if-condition   result clause

If Mary *were* more intelligent, she would learn faster.
  |
subjunctive

2. Expressions of wish

   I wish I *were* in Europe right now.
     |
   subjunctive

If only Mary *were* more intelligent.
|
subjunctive

3. Expressions of necessity or demand, often with verbs of asking, urging, demanding, requesting. This use requires a different form of the subjunctive.

It is necessary that he *be* here.
|
subjunctive

I asked that she *be* present.
|
subjunctive

In Italian: The subjunctive, called the **congiuntivo,** is used very frequently but unfortunately English usage will rarely help you decide where and how to use the subjunctive in Italian. We encourage you to memorize the verb forms of the four subjunctive tenses (present, imperfect, present perfect, and past perfect) and to learn the verbs, expressions and clauses which will require the use of a subjunctive verb form.

What is the Conditional?

Some modern English grammar books do not include the "conditional." It is an important mood in Italian, however. The use of the Italian **condizionale** and what we will call for our purposes the English "conditional" are sufficiently similar to justify a comparison.

The use of the conditional both in English and Italian does not necessarily mean that the sentence implies a "condition."

In English: The PRESENT CONDITIONAL is a compound tense. It is formed with the auxiliary WOULD + THE DICTIONARY FORM OF THE MAIN VERB.

> I said that I *would come* tomorrow.
> If she had the money, she *would call* him.
> I *would like* some ketchup, please.

Note: The auxiliary *would* in English has several meanings. It does not correspond to the conditional when it stands for *used to,* as in "She *would talk* while he painted." In this sentence, the verb means *used to* and requires the imperfect in Italian.

The PAST CONDITIONAL or CONDITIONAL PERFECT is composed of the auxiliary WOULD HAVE + THE PAST PARTICIPLE OF THE MAIN VERB.

> He *would have spoken,* if he had known the truth.
> If she had had the time, she *would have written* to him.
> I *would have eaten,* if I had been hungry.

The "conditional" is used in the following ways:

1. In the main clause of a hypothetical statement which is contrary-to-fact

> If I were rich, I *would buy* a Cadillac.

"I would buy a Cadillac" is called the MAIN CLAUSE, or RESULT CLAUSE. It is a clause because it is composed of a group of words containing a subject *(I)* and a verb *(would buy)* and is used as part of a sentence. It is the main clause because it expresses a complete thought and can stand by itself as a complete sentence.

"If I were rich" is called the SUBORDINATE CLAUSE, or *IF*-CLAUSE. Although it contains a subject *(I)* and a verb *(were)*, it does not express a complete thought and cannot stand alone.

2. In the subordinate clause to express a FUTURE IN THE PAST. (This means that the main clause must be in the past.)

He said that he *would come.*
    (1)   (2)

Action (2) of the subordinate clause takes place after action (1). Therefore, action (2) is a future in the past and takes the conditional.

If the main clause is in the present, then the future tense is used to express a future action.

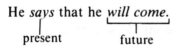

He *says* that he *will come.*
   present   future

3. As a polite form with *like* and as a "softened" command form

I *would like* to eat.

   This is more "polite" than
   "I want to eat."

Would you please close the door.

   This command is "softened" by
   the use of *would.*

In Italian: You do not need an auxiliary to indicate the present conditional; it is a simple tense. It is formed with the FUTURE STEM (see p. 75) + CONDITIONAL ENDINGS.

- of regular verbs

Infinitive	Stem	+	Conditional endings	
parl**are**	parler-		parler**ei**	*I would speak*
tem**ere**	temer-		temer**ebbe**	*he would fear*
part**ire**	partir-		partir**emmo**	*we would leave*

- of irregular verbs

Infinitive	Stem	+	Conditional endings	
av**ere**	avr-		avr**ei**	*I would have*
vol**ere**	vorr-		vorr**ebbe**	*he would want*

The past conditional or conditional perfect is formed by putting the auxiliary verb *AVERE* OR *ESSERE* IN THE PRESENT CONDITIONAL + THE PAST PARTICIPLE OF THE MAIN VERB.

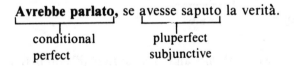

Avrebbe parlato, se avesse saputo la verità.
conditional perfect   pluperfect subjunctive

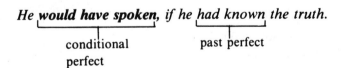

He would have spoken, if he had known the truth.
conditional perfect   past perfect

Let us study more examples of constructions using the conditional, so that you learn to recognize them and to use the appropriate Italian tense.

1. Sequence of tenses in hypothetical statements:

Hypothetical statements are easy to recognize because they are always made up of two clauses:

   a) the "if" clause; that is, the subordinate clause that starts with *if* (**se** in Italian)
   b) the result clause; that is, the main clause (see p. 169).

Hypothetical statements can require the indicative or the conditional depending on whether you are expressing a possibility in the future or a condition which is contrary-to-fact at the present.

The following sentences contrast the tense sequence in English and Italian.

- a hypothetical statement which expresses a possibility

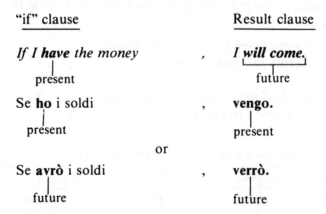

"if" clause		Result clause
*If I **have** the money*	,	*I **will come.***
present		future
Se **ho** i soldi	,	**vengo.**
present		present
or		
Se **avrò** i soldi	,	**verrò.**
future		future

- a hypothetical statement which is contrary-to-fact

   in the present:

"if" clause		Result clause
*If I **had** the money*	,	*I **would come.***
simple past		conditional

96

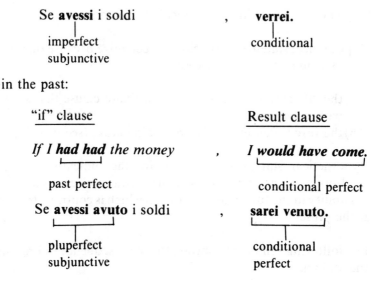

Se **avessi** i soldi , **verrei.**

imperfect
subjunctive
conditional

in the past:

"if" clause Result clause

*If I **had had** the money* , *I **would have come.***

past perfect conditional perfect

Se **avessi avuto** i soldi , **sarei venuto.**

pluperfect
subjunctive
conditional
perfect

In English and in Italian the "if" clause can come either at the beginning of the sentence before the main clause, or at the end of the sentence.

*I **would come,** if I **had** the money.*
Verrei, se **avessi** i soldi.

*If I **had** the money, I **would come.***
Se **avessi** i soldi, **verrei.**

Here is a reference chart of the sequence of tenses.

English		Italian	
"if" clause	Result clause	"if" clause	Result clause
present + future		present + present or future + future	
simple past + conditional		imperfect subjunctive + conditional	
past perfect + conditional perfect		pluperfect + conditional subjunctive perfect	

2. The conditional perfect is used in the subordinate clause to express a future in the past. English uses the simple conditional in this type of subordinate clause.

Identify the English tense and use the Italian equivalent.

- *He said that he **would come** the next day.*

    past   conditional

Ha detto che **sarebbe venuto** il giorno dopo.

   present   conditional
   perfect   perfect

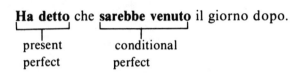

- *You **promised** that you **would do** it.*

    past   conditional

Hai promesso che lo **avresti fatto.**

   present   conditional
   perfect   perfect

3. The conditional as a polite form with *like* and as a "softened" command form.

- *I **would like** to go out this evening.*

  conditional infinitive

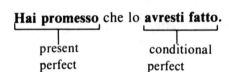

Instead of: I want to go out this evening.

Mi **piacerebbe** uscire stasera.

  conditional infinitive

- *Would you bring me a glass of water, please?*

conditional

Instead of: Bring me a glass of water.

Mi **porterebbe** un bicchiere d'acqua, per favore?

conditional

What is a Reflexive Verb?

A REFLEXIVE VERB is a verb conjugated with a special pronoun called a REFLEXIVE PRONOUN; some textbook explanations say that the pronoun serves to "reflect" the action of the verb on the performer or subject.

> *She* cut *herself* with the knife.
>
> *He* saw *himself* in the mirror.

In English: The pronouns which end with *-self* or *-selves* are used to make verbs reflexive. Here are the reflexive pronouns.

myself	ourselves
yourself	yourselves
himself	
herself	themselves
itself	

Observe their usage in the following examples:

I cut *myself.*

You dried *yourself* with a towel.

Paul and Mary blamed *themselves* for the accident.

In Italian: The reflexive pronouns are:

mi	*myself*
ti	*yourself (fam. sing.)*
si	*himself, herself, yourself (form. sing.)*
ci	*ourselves*
vi	*yourselves (fam. pl.)*
si	*themselves, yourselves (form. pl.)*

Certain verbs in Italian are reflexive verbs. Reflexive verbs have an infinitive form which has the reflexive pronoun **si** attached to the end: **lavarsi** *(to wash oneself).* In the dictionary the infinitive is listed as **lavarsi** which is a separate verb from **lavare** *(to wash).* Since the reflexive pronoun reflects the action of the verb on the performer, the reflexive pronoun will change as the subject changes. When you learn to conjugate a reflexive verb, you will need to memorize the conjugation with the reflexive pronouns. Let's look at the conjugation of **lavarsi** *(to wash oneself)* in the present tense; it is a regular **-are** verb and it is a reflexive verb.

Subject pronoun	Reflexive pronoun	Verb form
io	mi	lavo
tu	ti	lavi
lui lei Lei	si	lava
noi	ci	laviamo
voi	vi	lavate
loro Loro	si	lavano

Reflexive verbs can be conjugated in all tenses. The subject pronoun and reflexive pronoun remain the same regardless of the verb tense; only the verb form changes: **lui si laverà** *(he will wash),* **si è lavato** *(he washed).*

The perfect tenses of reflexive verbs are always conjugated with the auxiliary **essere** and the past participle agrees in gender and number with the subject.

> I bambini **si sono lavati.**
> *The children washed.*

> Maria **si è vestita** in fretta.
> *Mary got dressed in a hurry.*

Reflexive verbs are more common in Italian than in English; that is, there are many verbs that take a reflexive pronoun in Italian though not in English. For example, when you say in English, "Robert shaved" it is understood, but not stated, that "Robert shaved himself." In Italian the "himself" has to be stated. The English verb *to get up* also has a reflexive meaning: "Mary got up" means that she got herself up. In Italian you express *to get up* by using the verb **alzarsi,** that is **alzare** *(to raise)* + the reflexive pronoun **si** *(oneself).*

There are many expressions in English such as *to have a good time, to get dressed, to sit down* which are not reflexive but in Italian require the use of a reflexive verb **(divertirsi, vestirsi, sedersi).** You will need to memorize these reflexive verbs along with the reflexive pronoun.

What is Meant by Active and Passive Voice?

ACTIVE VOICE and PASSIVE VOICE are terms used to describe the relationship between the verb and its subject.

In English:

The ACTIVE VOICE. A verb is active when it expresses an action performed by the subject.

> John reads the newspaper.
> S   V   DO

> The girl closes the window.
>   S   V   DO

> Lightning strikes the tree.
>   S   V   DO

In all these examples the subject (S) performs the action of the verb (V) and the direct object (DO) is the receiver of the action.

The PASSIVE VOICE. A verb is passive when it expresses an action performed on the subject.

> The newspaper is read by John.
>   S   V   Agent

> The window is closed by the girl.
>   S   V   Agent

The tree is struck by lightning.

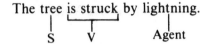

In all these examples, the subject is not the performer of the action but is having the action performed upon it. Note also that the tense of the sentence is indicated by the tense of the auxiliary *to be:* "The newspaper *is* read by John" is in the present tense; whereas, "The newspaper *was* read by John" is in the past tense.

When an active sentence is changed into a passive one the following occurs:

1. The direct object of the active sentence becomes the subject of the passive sentence.

2. The subject of the active sentence becomes the agent of the passive sentence (although the agent is often omitted) and is introduced by *by.*

In Italian: An active sentence can be changed to the passive just as in English.

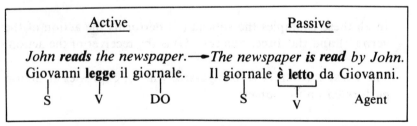

You should note that

- All verbs in the passive are made up of a form of the auxiliary verb *ESSERE* + THE PAST PARTICIPLE OF THE MAIN VERB and the agent is introduced by **da** *(by).*

Il giornale **è letto** da Giovanni.

Agent

- The tense of the passive voice is indicated by the tense of the auxiliary verb **essere.**

La finestra **è** chiusa dalla ragazza.
|
present

*The window **is** closed by the girl.*
|
present

La finestra **è stata** chiusa dalla ragazza.
|___|
present perfect

*The window **was** closed by the girl.*
|
past

La finestra **sarà** chiusa dalla ragazza.
|
future

*The window **will be** closed by the girl.*
|___|
future

- Because the auxiliary verb in the passive is always **essere,** the past participles must agree in gender and number with the subject of the sentence.

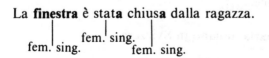

La **finestra** è stata chiusa dalla ragazza.
fem. sing.   fem. sing.   fem. sing.

The window was closed by the girl.

I **turisti** sono bene accolti dagli italiani.

masc. pl.   masc. pl.

Tourists are well received by Italians.

Although Italian has a passive voice it does not favor its use as English does. It is used infrequently, and generally in the past tenses. Italian speakers avoid the passive, particularly when the doer of the action is unimportant. They use the **si**-construction instead.

The *SI*-CONSTRUCTION

In order to use the **si**-construction as a replacement for the passive voice:

1. Determine in the English passive sentence whether the subject is singular or plural.

   • If it is singular, the **si**- construction will take a third person singular verb.

   • If it is plural, the **si**- construction will take a third person plural verb.

2. Place the subject of the sentence after the verb in Italian.

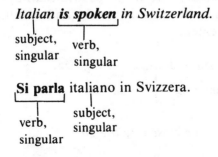

Italian **is spoken** *in Switzerland.*

subject, singular   verb, singular

Si parla italiano in Svizzera.

verb, singular   subject, singular

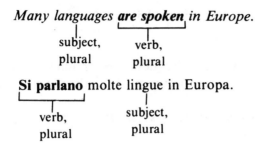

Note: Remember that the passive voice is not used very often in Italian, so that you would rarely hear the sentences:

L'italiano è parlato in Svizzera.
Molte lingue sono parlate in Europa.

You should use instead the **si-** construction, as in the above examples.

What is an Adjective?

An ADJECTIVE is a word which describes or limits a noun or a pronoun. It is said that the adjective modifies the noun or pronoun.

In English: Adjectives may be classified in several ways:

- DESCRIPTIVE ADJECTIVES indicate a quality of the noun

   She lived in a *large* house.
   He has *brown* eyes.

- POSSESSIVE ADJECTIVES indicate ownership or relationship (see p. 115)

   His book is lost.
   Our parents are away.

- INTERROGATIVE ADJECTIVES ask a question about the noun (see p. 122)

   What book is lost?
   Which newspaper do you want?

- DEMONSTRATIVE ADJECTIVES indicate or specify the noun (see p. 124)

   This teacher is excellent.
   That question is very appropriate.

Descriptive adjectives are divided into two groups depending on how they are joined to the noun they modify.

1. An ATTRIBUTIVE ADJECTIVE is joined directly to its noun and always precedes it.

The *good* children were praised.

noun

A *small* house is comfortable.

noun

2. A **PREDICATE ADJECTIVE** is joined to its noun (the subject of the sentence) by a linking verb, usually a form of *to be.*

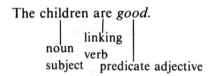

The children are *good.*

noun   linking verb

subject   predicate adjective

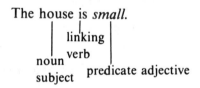

The house is *small.*

linking verb

noun subject   predicate adjective

You should also be able to recognize **NOUNS USED AS ADJECTIVES;** that is, a noun used to modify another noun.

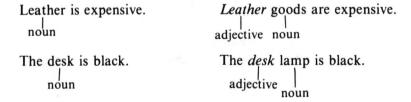

Leather is expensive.   *Leather* goods are expensive.

noun   adjective noun

The desk is black.   The *desk* lamp is black.

noun   adjective noun

In Italian: Adjectives are identified in the same way as in English. The most important difference is that the adjective must always agree with the noun it modifies; that is, it must correspond in gender and number with its noun. Thus, the form of an adjective depends on whether the noun is masculine or feminine, singular or plural.

the red dress	il vestito **rosso**
the red dresses	i vestiti **rossi**
the red car	la macchina **rossa**
the red cars	le macchine **rosse**

As in English, there are attributive adjectives and predicate adjectives.

1. Attributive adjectives generally follow the noun they modify. However, there is a small group of very commonly used attributive adjectives which normally precede the noun. Your Italian textbook will identify these adjectives.

   Una casa **piccola** è comoda.
   *A **small** house is comfortable.*

   I **buoni** bambini erano lodati.
   *The **good** children were praised.*

2. Predicate adjectives always modify the noun which is the subject of the sentence and agree with it in number and gender.

I bambini sono **buoni.**

masc. pl.   masc. pl.

*The children are **good.***

La casa è **piccola.**

fem. sing   fem. sing.

*The house is **small.***

Unlike English, a noun may not be used as an adjective. In Italian, a noun may be used to modify another noun only by means of a prepositional phrase (preposition + noun).

***leather** goods*	prodotti **in pelle**
***desk** lamp*	lampada **da tavolo**

As you can see in these examples, agreement is not required between the noun in the prepositional phrase and the noun modified.

Because of their importance and complexity, possessive adjectives, interrogative adjectives and demonstrative adjectives are discussed in separate sections.

What is Meant by Comparison of Adjectives?

We make a comparison of adjectives when two or more nouns have the same quality and we want to indicate a greater, lesser or equal degree of this quality.

There are three degrees of the descriptive adjectives: POSITIVE, COMPARATIVE and SUPERLATIVE.

Positive	Comparative	Superlative
tall	taller	tallest
pretty	prettier	prettiest
intelligent	more intelligent	most intelligent
expensive	less expensive	least expensive

In English: Let us examine in more detail what is meant by the different degrees of an adjective and how each degree is formed.

1. The POSITIVE is the basic form of the adjective. It indicates the quality of a person or thing without reference to another person or thing.

    John is *tall.*
    Mary is *pretty.*
    This child is *intelligent.*
    My car is *expensive.*

2. The COMPARATIVE indicates a greater degree (superiority), a lesser degree (inferiority) or an equal degree (equality) of the quality of a person or thing compared with another.

    The comparison of superiority is formed:

    • by SHORT ADJECTIVE + *-ER* + *THAN*

    John is *taller than* Robert.
    Mary is *prettier than* Susan.

● by *MORE* + LONGER ADJECTIVE + *THAN*

This child is *more intelligent than* his friend.
My car is *more expensive than* your car.

The comparison of inferiority is formed:

● by *LESS* + ADJECTIVE + *THAN*

Robert is *less tall than* John.
Your car is *less expensive than* my car.

The comparison of equality is formed:

● by *AS* + ADJECTIVE + *AS*

John is *as tall as* Robert.
My car is *as expensive as* your car.

3. The **SUPERLATIVE** indicates the highest degree of a quality with reference to more than one other person or thing.

The superlative of superiority is formed:

● by *THE* + SHORT ADJECTIVE + *-EST*

John is *the tallest* of the three brothers.
Mary is *the prettiest* of all.

● by *THE* + *MOST* + LONGER ADJECTIVE

This child is *the most intelligent* in the class.
My car is *the most expensive* in the race.

The superlative of inferiority is formed:

● by *THE* + *LEAST* + ADJECTIVE

Robert is *the least tall* of the three brothers.
My car is *the least expensive* in the race.

A few adjectives do not follow this regular pattern of comparison. You must use an entirely different form for the comparative and the superlative.

This apple is *bad.*	(positive)
This apple is *worse.* not *badder	(comparative)
This apple is the *worst.* not *baddest	(superlative)

In Italian: There are the same three degrees of adjectives as in English: positive, comparative and superlative. Remember that agreement between the adjective and the noun is always required.

1. The positive is the basic form of the adjective.

Giovanni è **alto.**
*John is **tall.***

Maria è **carina.**
*Mary is **pretty.***

Questo bambino è **intelligente.**
*This child is **intelligent.***

La mia macchina è **cara.**
*My car is **expensive.***

2. The comparative of superiority or inferiority is formed:

- by $\left\{ \begin{array}{l} \text{(sup.)} \ \textit{PIÙ} \\ \text{(inf.)} \ \textit{MENO} \end{array} \right\}$ + ADJECTIVE + *DI*

---

*An asterisk means that what follows is ungrammatical.

Giovanni è **più alto di** Roberto.
*John is **taller than** Robert.*

Roberto è **meno alto di** Giovanni.
*Robert is **less tall than** John.*

La mia macchina è **più cara della** tua macchina.
*My car is **more expensive than** your car.*

La tua macchina è **meno cara della** mia macchina.
*Your car is **less expensive than** my car.*

The comparative of equality is formed:

• by $\left.\begin{array}{c} \textit{(TANTO)} \\ \textit{(COSÌ)} \end{array}\right\}$ + ADJECTIVE + $\left\{\begin{array}{l} \textit{QUANTO} \\ \textit{COME} \end{array}\right.$

Giovanni è **(tanto) alto quanto** Roberto.
*John is **as tall as** Robert.*

La mia macchina è **(così) cara come** la tua macchina.
*My car is **as expensive as** your car.*

3. The superlative of superiority and inferiority is formed:

• by DEFINITE ARTICLE + $\left\{\begin{array}{ll} \text{(sup.)} & \textit{PIÙ} \\ \text{(inf.)} & \textit{MENO} \end{array}\right\}$ + ADJECTIVE + *DI*

Giovanni è **il più alto dei** tre fratelli.
*John is **the tallest of the** three brothers.*

Questo bambino è **il più intelligente della** classe.
*This child is **the most intelligent in the** class.*

Roberto è **il meno alto dei** tre fratelli.
*Robert is **the least tall of the** three brothers.*

La mia macchina è **la meno cara della** corsa.
*My car is **the least expensive in the race.***

A few adjectives have irregular forms of comparison in addition to the regular forms.

Questa mela è **cattiva.**   (positive)
*This apple is **bad.***

Questa mela è $\left\{ \begin{array}{l} \textbf{più cattiva.} \\ \textbf{peggiore.} \end{array} \right.$ (comparative)

*This apple is **worse.***

Questa mela è $\left\{ \begin{array}{l} \textbf{la più cattiva.} \\ \textbf{la peggiore.} \end{array} \right.$ (superlative)

*This apple is **the worst.***

Note: Adverbs (see **What is an Adverb?**, p. 127) are compared in the same manner as adjectives in both English and Italian.

What is a Possessive Adjective?

A POSSESSIVE ADJECTIVE indicates ownership of, or relationship to, the noun it modifies (*my* books, *their* friends, *our* mother). The owner or the relating person is called the "possessor," and the noun modified is called the person or item "possessed."

In English: Here is a list of the possessive adjectives:

> my
> your
> his, her, its
> our
> your
> their

The possessive adjective refers only to the possessor and has no grammatical relationship with the person(s) or item(s) possessed.

> *I* am reading *my* magazines.

> *We* are selling *our* house.

> *Mario* is reading *his* magazines.

In Italian: The possessive adjective refers to the possessor and in addition must agree in gender and number with the person(s) or item(s) possessed.

> **Io** leggo **le mie riviste.**

> *I am reading **my** magazines.*

Le mie refers to the possessor **(io)**, but agrees in gender and number with the items possessed **(riviste).**

Noi vediamo spesso **le nostre sorelle.**

*We often see **our** sisters.*

Le nostre refers to the possessor **(noi)**, but agrees in gender and number with the persons possessed **(sorelle).**

Mario legge **le sue riviste.**

*Mario is reading **his** magazines.*

Le sue refers to the possessor **(Mario),** but agrees in gender and number with the items possessed **(riviste).**

Here is a chart of the Italian equivalents of the possessive adjectives.

Possessor	masculine singular	feminine singular	masculine plural	feminine plural
my	il mio	la mia	i miei	le mie
your (fam. sing.)	il tuo	la tua	i tuoi	le tue
his, her, its	il suo	la sua	i suoi	le sue
your (form. sing.)	il Suo	la Sua	i Suoi	le Sue
our	il nostro	la nostra	i nostri	le nostre
your (fam. pl.)	il vostro	la vostra	i vostri	le vostre
their	il loro	la loro	i loro	le loro
your (form. pl.)	il Loro	la Loro	i Loro	le Loro

Italian normally uses the definite article before the possessive adjective and the formal possessive adjectives are capitalized.

These are the steps you should follow in order to choose the correct possessive adjective and its proper form:

1. Identify the possessor.

2. Identify the gender and number of the person(s) or item(s) possessed.

3. Choose the Italian possessive adjective which corresponds to the possessor (found under step 1) and the gender and number of the possessed (found under step 2).

Below are examples of how these steps are applied to sentences with each possible possessor.

- my

    *I have **my** books.*

    1. Possessor: *my*
    2. Gender and number of possessed: **Libri** *(books)* is masculine plural.
    3. Italian equivalent of *my:* **i miei** (masculine plural).

    Ho **i miei** libri.

- your

    In the case of the possessive adjective *your,* determine whether

    —it is appropriate to use the familiar or formal form of address (see **What is Meant by Familiar and Formal You?**, p. 34).

    —the *your* is addressed to one person (singular) or to more than one person (plural).

    *Is this **your** house?*   [You are addressing a child.]

    1. Possessor: *your*
       Formal or familiar: familiar
       Singular or plural: singular
    2. Gender and number of possessed: **Casa** *(house)* is feminine singular.
    3. Italian equivalent of *your:* **la tua** (familiar singular/feminine singular)

    È questa **la tua** casa?

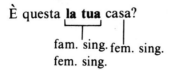

    fam. sing. fem. sing.
    fem. sing.

*Is this **your** house?*   [You are addressing more than one child.]

1. Possessor: *your*
   Formal or familiar: familiar
   Singular or plural: plural
2. Gender and number of possessed: **Casa** *(house)* is feminine singular.
3. Italian equivalent of *your:* **la vostra** (familiar plural/feminine singular)

È questa **la vostra** casa?

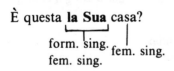

       fam. pl.   fem. sing.
       fem. sing.

*Is this **your** house?*   [You are addressing an adult.]

1. Possessor: *your*
   Formal or familiar: formal
   Singular or plural: singular
2. Gender and number of possessed: **Casa** *(house)* is feminine singular.
3. Italian equivalent of *your:* **la Sua** (formal singular/feminine singular)

È questa **la Sua** casa?

     form. sing. fem. sing.
     fem. sing.

*Is this **your** house?*   [You are addressing more than one
adult.]

1. Possessor: *your*
   Formal or familiar: formal
   Singular or plural: plural
2. Gender and number of possessed: **Casa** *(house)* is feminine singular.
3. Italian equivalent of *your:* **la Loro** (formal plural/feminine singular)

È questa **la Loro** casa?

       form. pl. fem. sing.
       fem. sing.

• his, her, its

*Mary reads **her** books.*

1. Possessor: *her*
2. Gender and number of possessed: **Libri** *(books)* is masculine plural.
3. Italian equivalent of *her:* **i suoi** (masculine plural)

Maria legge **i suoi** libri.

*Mario reads **his** books.*

1. Possessor: *his*
2. Gender and number of possessed: **Libri** *(books)* is masculine plural.
3. Italian equivalent of *his:* **i suoi** (masculine plural)

Mario legge **i suoi** libri.

Since the possessive adjective agrees with the items possessed **(libri),** the form of the adjective for both *his* and *her* is **i suoi.** The gender of the possessor (Maria or Mario) is not reflected in the Italian possessive adjective **i suoi** as it is in the English *his, her.* In Italian, only the context will identify the gender of the possessor.

- our

Our *house is downtown.*

1. Possessor: *our*
2. Gender and number of possessed: **Casa** *(house)* is feminine singular.
3. Italian equivalent of *our:* **la nostra** (feminine singular)

La nostra casa è in centro.

- their

This is **their** *house.*

1. Possessor: *their*
2. Gender and number of possessed: **Casa** *(house)* is feminine singular.
3. Italian equivalent of *their:* **la loro** (feminine singular)

Questa è **la loro** casa.

Since **loro** is invariable, the gender and number of the possessive adjective are indicated only by the definite article.

Queste sono **le loro** case.

|invariable|

fem. pl. fem. pl.

These are **their** *houses.*

In Italian and in English, the subject and the possessive adjectives do not necessarily match. It all depends on what you want to say.

- **Ha** il **mio** libro?
  3rd   1st
  per.   per.

  *Does **he** have **my** book?*
  3rd   1st
  per.   per.

- **Hai** portato **i loro** regali?
  2nd   3rd
  per.   per.

  *Did **you** bring **their** gifts?*
  2nd   3rd
  per.   per.

What is an Interrogative Adjective?

An INTERROGATIVE ADJECTIVE is a word which asks a question about a noun.

In English: The words *which, what* and *how much/how many* are called interrogative adjectives when they precede a noun and are used to ask a question.

> *What* courses are you taking?
> *Which* newspaper do you prefer to read?
> *How much* coffee do you drink?
> *How many* children were there?

In Italian: There are three interrogative adjectives: **che** corresponding to the English *what;* **quale/quali** corresponding to *which;* the forms of **quanto** corresponding to *how much/how many.*

- **Che** + noun? = *What* + noun?

> **Che** giornale leggi?
> *What newspaper do you read?*

> **Che** corsi frequenti?
> *What courses are you taking?*

Che is invariable; it does not agree in gender and number with the noun it modifies.

- **Quale/Quali** + noun? = *Which* + noun?

> **Quale** giornale preferisci leggere?
> |
> singular

> *Which newspaper do you prefer to read?*

Quali dischi porti?

plural

Which records are you bringing?

Quale agrees only in number with the noun it modifies.

Quale implies a choice between two or more alternatives whereas **che** is used in more general terms.

Quale giornale leggi?
Which newspaper do you read? [among these three]

Che giornale leggi?
What newspaper do you read? [in general]

- **Quanto (-a, -i, -e) + noun? =** *How much/How many + noun?*

Quanto has four forms to agree in gender and number with the noun it modifies.

Quanto caffè bevi?

masc. sing.

masc. sing.

How much coffee do you drink?

Quanta minestra vuoi?

fem. sing. fem. sing.

How much soup do you want?

Quanti bambini c'erano?

masc. pl. masc. pl.

How many children were there?

Quante valigie porti?
| |
fem. pl.   fem. pl.

*How **many** suitcases are you taking?*

What is a Demonstrative Adjective?

A DEMONSTRATIVE ADJECTIVE is a word used to point out a person or an object.

In English: The demonstrative adjectives are ***this/these*** which point out a person or an object near the speaker and ***that/those*** which point out a person or an object away from the speaker. They are a rare example of adjectives agreeing in number with the noun they modify: *this* changes to *these* before a plural noun and *that* changes to *those*.

    this cat ⟶ *these* cats   *that* man ⟶ *those* men

In Italian: There are two sets of demonstrative adjectives: one set for persons or objects close to the speaker, and one for those away from the speaker. Each set has four forms which agree in gender and number with the nouns they modify: a masculine and feminine form in the singular to agree with the singular nouns and a masculine and feminine form in the plural to agree with the plural nouns.

1. Forms used to point out a person or an object near the speaker:

questo (-a, -i, -e) = *this, these*

this boy	**questo** ragazzo	(masc. sing.)
this house	**questa** casa	(fem. sing.)
these boys	**questi** ragazzi	(masc. pl.)
these houses	**queste** case	(fem. pl.)

If you want to say "*this* boy" in Italian, begin by analyzing the Italian equivalent for the word "boy," which is **ragazzo**.

Do you see this boy?

Ragazzo is masculine singular, so that the word for *this* is also masculine singular.

Vedi **questo** ragazzo?

masc. sing.   masc. sing.

Similarly for "*these* houses" begin by analyzing the Italian equivalent for the word "houses," which is **case**.

Do you see these houses?

Case is feminine plural, so that the word for *these* is also feminine plural.

Vedi **queste** case?

fem. pl.   fem. pl.

2. Forms used to point out a person or object away from the speaker:

quello = *that, those*

Quello has irregularities in its forms which are similar to those of **di** combined with the definite article. (See **What is a Partitive?**, p. 17.) Therefore, the following examples do not include all the possible forms.

that student	**quello** studente	(masc. sing.)
that boy	**quel** ragazzo	(masc. sing.)
that house	**quella** casa	(fem. sing.)
those boys	**quei** ragazzi	(masc. pl.)
those houses	**quelle** case	(fem. pl.)

If you want to say "*that* boy" in Italian, begin by analyzing the Italian equivalent for "boy."

> *Do you see that boy?*

Ragazzo is masculine singular, so that the word for *that* is also masculine singular.

Vedi **quel** ragazzo?

masc. sing.   masc. sing.

Similarly, if you want to say "*those* houses" in Italian, begin by analyzing the Italian equivalent for "houses."

> *Do you see those houses?*

Case is feminine plural, so that the word for *those* is also feminine plural.

Vedi **quelle** case?

fem. pl.   fem. pl.

What is an Adverb?

An ADVERB is a word that modifies (describes) a verb, an adjective or another adverb. Adverbs indicate quantity, time, place, intensity and manner.

> Mary drives *well.*
> |
>   verb

> The house is *very* big.
> |
>   adjective

> The girl ran *too* quickly.
> |
>   adverb

In English: Here are some examples of adverbs:

- of quantity or degree

> Mary sleeps *little.*
> Bob is *quite* studious.

These adverbs answer the question *how much.*

- of time

> He will come *soon.*
> The children arrived *late.*

These adverbs answer the question *when.*

- of place

> The teacher looked *around.*
> The old were left *behind.*

These adverbs answer the question *where.*

- of intensity

  Bob *really* wants to learn Italian.
  Mary can *actually* read Latin.

  These adverbs are used for *emphasis*.

- of manner

  Bob sings *beautifully*.
  They parked the car *carefully*.

  These adverbs answer the question *how*. They are the most common adverbs and can usually be recognized by their *-ly* ending.

In Italian: You will have to memorize most adverbs as vocabulary items. Most adverbs of manner can be recognized by the ending **-mente** which corresponds to the English ending *-ly*.

naturalmente	*naturally*
generalmente	*generally*
rapidamente	*rapidly*

The most important thing for you to remember is that adverbs are invariable: this means that they never change. (Adverbs never become plural, nor do they have gender.) For this reason, it is necessary that you distinguish adverbs from adjectives which do change. When you write a sentence in Italian, always make sure that the adjectives agree with the noun or pronoun they modify and that adverbs remain unchanged.

- *The tall girl talked rapidly.*

  Tall modifies the noun *girl;* it is an adjective.
  Rapidly modifies the verb *talked;* it describes how she talked; it is an adverb.

  La **ragazza alta** parlò **rapidamente.**

  fem. sing.

- *The **tall** boy talked **rapidly**.*

    Tall modifies the noun *boy;* it is an adjective.
    Rapidly modifies the verb *talked;* it describes how he talked; it is an adverb.

    Il ragazzo alto parlò rapidamente.

    masc. sing.

Note: Remember that in English *good* is an adjective; *well* is an adverb.

    The boy is *good.*   (He isn't bad.)

    Good modifies *boy;* it is therefore an adjective.

    The boy is *well.*   (He isn't sick.)

    Well modifies *is;* it is therefore an adverb.

Likewise, in Italian **buono** is an adjective meaning *good;* **bene** is the adverb meaning *well.*

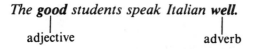

    *The **good** students speak Italian **well.***
       adjective   adverb

    I **buoni** studenti parlano **bene** l'italiano.
       masc. pl.   adverb

Adverbs are compared in the same manner as adjectives; that is, they have three degrees (see **What is Meant by Comparison of Adjectives?, p. 110).

130

What is a Preposition?

A **PREPOSITION** is a word which shows the relationship of one word (usually a noun or pronoun) to another in the sentence. The noun or pronoun following the preposition is called the **OBJECT OF THE PREPOSITION**. The preposition plus its object is called a **PREPOSITIONAL PHRASE**. Prepositions normally indicate position, direction or time.

In English: Here are examples of some prepositions showing:

- position

    Bob was *in* the car.
    The books are *on* the table.

- direction

    Mary went *to* school.
    The students came directly *from* class.

- time

    Italian people go on vacation *in* August.
    Their son will be home *at* Christmas.

Not all prepositions are single words:

| because of | contrary to | in front of |
| due to | in spite of | on account of |

In Italian: You will have to memorize prepositions as vocabulary items. Their meaning and use must be carefully studied. There are three important things to remember:

1. Prepositions are invariable. This means that they never change. (They never become plural, nor do they have a gender.)

2. Every language uses prepositions differently. Do not assume that the same preposition is used in Italian as in English or that when a preposition is needed in English it will also be needed in Italian and vice versa.

English	Italian

change of preposition

to laugh *at*	ridersi **di** *(of)*
to hear *on the* radio	ascoltare **alla** *(at)* radio

preposition ⟶ no preposition

to look *for*	cercare
to wait *for*	aspettare
to pay *for*	pagare
to go *on*	procedere

no preposition ⟶ preposition

to enter	entrare **in**
to telephone	telefonare **a**
to trust	fidarsi **di**
to approach	avvicinarsi **a**

A good dictionary will usually give you the verb plus the preposition when required.

Especially in the case of an English verb + preposition (PREPOSITIONAL VERBS), be careful not to translate literally into Italian. For example, when you consult the dictionary for *look for,* do not stop at the first entry for *look* which is **guardare** and then add the preposition **per** corresponding to *for.* Continue searching for the specific form *look for* which corresponds to the verb **cercare,** used without a preposition. So "I am looking for Frank" is not *"Guardo per Franco" but "Cerco Franco."

---

*An asterisk means that what follows is ungrammatical.

On the other hand, when looking up verbs such as *enter, telephone, trust,* be sure to include the Italian preposition which you find listed in the entry. So "Mary is entering the classroom" is not *"Maria entra la classe" but "Maria entra **in** classe."

3. Often spoken English places the preposition at the end of the sentence. Formal English places the preposition within the sentence or at the beginning of a question.

Spoken English	Formal English
The man I speak *to.* ⟶	The man *to* whom I speak.
Who are you playing *with?*	*With* whom are you playing?
The teacher I'm talking *about.*	The teacher *about* whom I'm talking.

Italian reflects the structure of formal English: it places the preposition within the sentence or at the beginning of a question.

L'uomo **a cui** parlo.
*The man **to whom** I speak.*

Con chi giocate?
***With whom** are you playing?*

There are some English expressions where the natural position of the preposition is at the end of the sentence; it is not a question of spoken or written language.

They don't understand what he is talking *about.*

Changing the structure by placing the preposition within the sentence may sound awkward.

They don't understand *about what* he is talking.

---

* An asterisk means that what follows is ungrammatical.

However, as awkward as it may sound in English, this is the structure to be used in the Italian sentence:

Loro non capiscono **di che cosa** stia parlando.
*They don't understand **about what** he is talking.*

In Italian, it is not possible to place a preposition at the end of a sentence.

Note: A special word needs to be said about the preposition **di** *(of)* in Italian, because it is used in structures that do not exist in English.

1. When a noun is used as an adjective to describe another noun (see p. 109) **di** is used as follows:

● THE NOUN DESCRIBED + *DI* + THE DESCRIBING NOUN USED WITH-OUT AN ARTICLE

    A   B
    i libri **di** chimica   *the chemistry books*
    l'olio **di** semi   *the vegetable oil*
    la statua **di** marmo   *the marble statue*
    la pioggia **di** primavera   *the spring rain*

The noun in column B describes the noun in column A.

2. When a noun relates to another noun in terms of possession or ownership (see p. 20)

● *DI* + DEFINITE ARTICLE + NOUN

    le macchine **del** signore   *the man's cars*
    le macchine **dei** signori   *the men's cars*

● *DI* + NAME

    le macchine **di** Giovanni   *John's cars*
    la casa **di** Maria Rossi   *Maria Rossi's house*

What is a Conjunction?

A CONJUNCTION is a word which joins words, phrases, or clauses.

Paul plays basketball *and* tennis.
We are going over the river *and* through the woods.
I liked *neither* the book *nor* the play.
The children are happy *whenever* he comes.

There are two kinds of conjunctions: coordinating and subordinating.

1. COORDINATING CONJUNCTIONS join words, phrases, and clauses that are equal; they *coordinate* elements of equal rank.

good *or* evil
over the river *and* through the woods
They invited us, *but* we couldn't go.

2. SUBORDINATING CONJUNCTIONS join a clause to the main clause; they *subordinate* one clause to another. Clauses introduced by a subordinating conjunction are called SUBORDINATE CLAUSES.

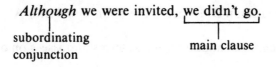

Although we were invited, we didn't go.

subordinating
conjunction

main clause

They left *because* they were bored.

main
clause

subordinating
conjunction

He said *that* he was tired.

main
clause

subordinating
conjunction

Notice that the main clause is not always the first clause of the sentence.

In English: The major coordinating conjunctions are *and, but, or, in fact,* and *therefore.* Typical subordinating conjunctions are *before, after, since, although, because, if, unless, so that, while, that,* and *when.* Some of these exist as both prepositons and subordinating conjunctions.

Look at the following examples where *before* and *after* are used both as a preposition and as a subordinating conjunction. When they introduce a clause they are functioning as a conjunction; when they do not, they are functioning as a preposition.

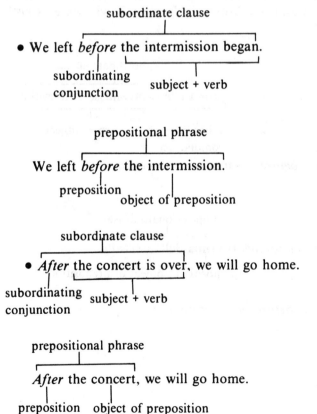

In Italian: Conjunctions are to be memorized as vocabulary items. Remember that like adverbs and prepositions, conjunctions are invariable; they never change. (They never become plural, nor do they have a gender.)

The major coordinating conjunctions are **e** *(and)*, **ma** *(but)*, **o** *(or)*, **infatti** *(in fact)*, and **dunque** *(therefore)*.

Some common subordinating conjunctions are **prima che** *(before)*, **dopo che** *(after)*, **poiché** *(since)*, **sebbene** *(although)*, **perché** *(because)*, **se** *(if)*, **a meno che** *(unless)*, **affinché** *(so that)*, **mentre** *(while)*, **che** *(that)*, and **quando** *(when)*.

You cannot assume that when the same word serves as both conjunction and preposition in English, it will serve as both in Italian.

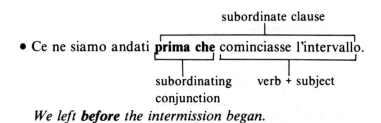

*We left **before** the intermission began.*

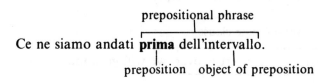

*We left **before** the intermission.*

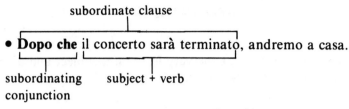

subordinate clause

• **Dopo che** il concerto sarà terminato, andremo a casa.

subordinating subject + verb
conjunction

After the concert is over, we will go home.

prepositional phrase

Dopo il concerto, andremo a casa.

preposition object of preposition

After the concert, we will go home.

These examples point out the importance of understanding the difference between a conjunction **(prima che, dopo che)** and a preposition **(prima, dopo).** Again, as you study vocabulary items, along with their meaning(s), you should always be aware of the function they have as a part of speech.

What are Objects?

Every sentence consists, at the very least, of a subject and a verb. This is called the SENTENCE BASE.

John writes.
She spoke.

The subject of the sentence base is a noun or pronoun. However, more complex sentences contain other nouns or pronouns which function as OBJECTS. They indicate the person(s) or thing(s) that receive the action of the verb.

John writes a letter.
subject   verb   object

She spoke to me.
subject   verb   object

There are three types of objects categorized according to the way they are related to the verb.

1. direct object
2. indirect object
3. object of preposition

In English:

1. DIRECT OBJECT: It receives the action of the verb directly, without a preposition relating it to the verb.

It answers the question *WHAT* OR *WHOM?* ASKED AFTER THE VERB.

- John writes *a letter.*

  John writes what? A letter.
  A letter is the direct object.

- They met *Mary.*

  They met whom? Mary.
  Mary is the direct object.

Do not assume that any word which follows a verb directly is automatically the direct object. It must answer the question *what?* or *whom?*

  John wrote yesterday.

  John wrote *what?* No answer.
  John wrote *whom?* No answer.
  John wrote *when?* Yesterday.

There is no direct object in the sentence. *Yesterday* does not answer the question *what?* or *whom?* (*Yesterday* is an adverb.)

2. INDIRECT OBJECT: It receives the action of the verb indirectly with the preposition "to" relating it to the verb.

   It answers the question *TO WHOM?* OR *TO WHAT?* ASKED AFTER THE VERB.

   - She wrote *to her friends.*

     She wrote to whom? To her friends.
     To her friends is the indirect object.

   - He gave a painting *to the museum.*

     He gave a painting to what? To the museum.
     To the museum is the indirect object.

The indirect object is normally related to the verb without the preposition *to* when it comes between the verb and the direct object.

John writes a letter *to his brother.*

or

John writes *his brother* a letter.

His brother answers the question *to whom?* and is the indirect object of the sentence even if the preposition "to" does not appear.

3. OBJECT OF PREPOSITION: It also receives the action of the verb indirectly with a preposition other than "to" relating it to the verb.

It answers the question made up of the PREPOSITION + *WHAT* OR *WHOM? (with what* or *whom?, for what* or *whom?, by what* or *whom?,* etc.) ASKED AFTER THE VERB.

• John went *with Mary.*

John went with whom? With Mary.
Mary is the object of the preposition *with.*

• He is working *for Mr. Jones.*

He is working for whom? For Mr. Jones.
Mr. Jones is the object of the preposition *for.*

In Italian: Direct and indirect objects and objects of prepositions are related to the verb in the same way as they are in English.

1. Direct object

• Giovanni scrive **una lettera.**
*John writes **a letter.***

- Hanno conosciuto **Maria.**
  *They met **Mary.***

2. Indirect object: It is always preceded by the preposition **a** except when the object is a pronoun. (See **What is an Object Pronoun?**, p. 146.)

   - Ha scritto **ai suoi amici.**
     *She wrote **to her friends.***

   - Ha donato un quadro **al museo.**
     *He gave a painting **to the museum.***

3. Object of preposition

   - Giovanni è andato **con Maria.**
     *John went **with Mary.***

   - Lavora **per il Signor Jones.**
     *He is working **for Mr. Jones.***

It should be pointed out that the relationship between verb and object often differs in English and Italian; thus, the object function also differs. For example, a verb may take an object of preposition in English but a direct object in Italian, or a direct object in English but an indirect object in Italian. For this reason, the function of an object must be established within the language in which you are working.

Here are some examples of the changes in function which you are most likely to encounter.

1. Object of a preposition in English —► Direct object in Italian

   *I am looking **for the book.***
   Function in English: Object of preposition
   I am looking for what? For the book.
   The book is the object of the preposition *for.*

Cerco il libro.

> Function in Italian: Direct object
> Che cerco? Il libro.
> Since **cercare** is not followed by a preposition,
> the object is direct.

Here is a list of a few common verbs which require an object of preposition in English and a direct object in Italian.

to look for	cercare
to look at	guardare
to wait for	aspettare
to pay for	pagare

2. Direct object in English——▶Indirect object in Italian

She calls her friends every day.

> Function in English: Direct object
> Whom does she call every day? Her friends.
> *Her friends* is the direct object.

Telefona ai suoi amici ogni giorno.

> Function in Italian: Indirect object
> A chi telefona ogni giorno? Ai suoi amici.
> The verb is **telefonare a** and takes an indirect object.

Here is a list of a few common verbs which require a direct object in English and an indirect object in Italian.

to call, telephone	telefonare **a**
to obey	obbedire **a**
to resemble	somigliare **a**
to approach	avvicinarsi **a**

3. Direct object in English⟶Object of a preposition in Italian

*Mary's parents remember **the war**.*

> Function in English: Direct object
> Mary's parents remember what? The war.
> *The war* is the direct object.

I genitori di Maria si ricordano **della guerra.**

di + la

> Function in Italian: Object of preposition
> Di che si ricordano i genitori di Maria? Della guerra.
> The verb is **ricordarsi di** and takes an object of a preposition.

Here is a list of a few common verbs which require a direct object in English and an object of a preposition in Italian.

to enter	entrare **in**
to trust	fidarsi **di**
to remember	ricordarsi **di**
to doubt	dubitare **di**

4. Subject in English ⟶Indirect object in Italian

With some Italian verbs (V) the equivalent of a subject (S) in English is an indirect object (IO) in Italian and the equivalent of a direct object (DO) in English is a subject (S) in Italian.

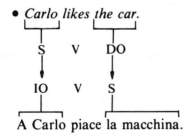

- *Carlo likes the car.*

S V DO

IO V S

A Carlo piace la macchina.

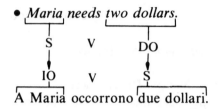

• *Maria needs two dollars.*

A Maria occorrono due dollari.

Let us go over this type of transformation step by step:

1. Transform the English sentence by turning the subject (S) into an indirect object (IO) and the direct object (DO) into the subject (S), using "is pleasing" instead of "likes."

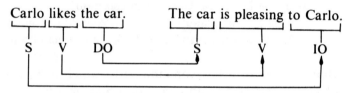

Carlo likes the car.   The car is pleasing to Carlo.

S   V   DO   S   V   IO

2. Place the indirect object at the beginning of the sentence.

* To Carlo is pleasing the car.

IO   V   S

3. Express the transformed sentence in Italian.

* *To Carlo is pleasing the car.*

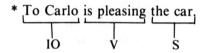

A Carlo piace la macchina.

IO   V   S

Here is a list of the common verbs which require an indirect object in Italian where English uses a subject.

to like	piacere
to be sorry, dislike	dispiacere
to need	occorrere
to be lacking, missing	mancare

---

* An asterisk means that the sentence is ungrammatical.

Always keep in mind when dealing with the above four categories that the function of the word must be identified within the Italian sentence, not the English sentence.

Objects in summary:

The different types of objects in a sentence are identified according to whether or not they are introduced by a preposition and if so, by which one.

The object which receives the action of the verb directly, without a preposition, is called direct.

The object which receives the action of the verb indirectly, through the preposition *to,* is called indirect.

The object which receives the action of the verb indirectly, through a preposition other than *to,* is called object of a preposition.

Your ability to recognize the three kinds of objects is essential when using pronouns. Different pronouns are used for the English pronoun *him,* for example, depending on whether *him* is a direct object **(lo),** an indirect object **(gli),** or the object of a preposition **(lui).** Always keep in mind that the function of the object pronoun must be identified within the Italian sentence, not within the English sentence.

What is an Object Pronoun?

Pronouns in English and in Italian change according to their function in the sentence. The pronouns used as subject of a sentence are studied in detail on p. 32. This chapter deals mainly with pronouns used as objects.

In English: The pronouns that function as objects in a sentence are called OBJECT PRONOUNS. Their form differs from that of subject pronouns. Object pronouns are used when a pronoun is a direct object, an indirect object, or an object of preposition (see p. 138).

He works for the newspaper.
subject
pronoun

Mother saw *him* last night.
direct object
pronoun

I lent my car to *him*.
indirect object
pronoun

They went to the movies with *him*.
object of preposition
pronoun

Compare the English pronouns:

Subject	Object
I	me
you	you
{ he	{ him
she	her
it	it
we	us
you	you
they	them

The form of the object pronoun is identical whether the pronoun is used as a direct object, indirect object, or an object of preposition.

In Italian: Normally the form of the pronoun changes according to its function in the sentence:

1. Direct object
2. Indirect object
3. Object of preposition

1. Direct object pronouns

1st pers. sing.	*me*	mi
2nd pers.	*you (fam.)*	ti
3rd pers.	{ *him, it (m.)*	lo
	her, it (f.)	la
	you (form. m. and f.)	La
1st pers. pl.	*us*	ci
2nd pers.	*you (fam.)*	vi
3rd pers.	*them (m.)*	li
	them (f.)	le
	you (form. m.)	Li
	you (form f.)	Le

The direct object pronouns are used as they are in English, but precede the conjugated verb.

- *John sees **me**.*

  John sees whom? Me.
  Me is the direct object pronoun.

  Giovanni **mi** vede.
  |
  direct object
  pronoun

- *John sees **us**.*

  John sees whom? Us.
  Us is the direct object pronoun.

  Giovanni **ci** vede.
  |
  direct object
  pronoun

- *John sees **him**.*

  John sees whom? Him.
  Him is the direct object pronoun.

  Giovanni **lo** vede.
  |
  direct object
  pronoun

You will need to pay special attention to the equivalent of English *it, them* and *you* (formal).

- it, them

  Remember that there are no neuter nouns in Italian: the equivalent of *it* and *them* will be masculine or feminine, depending on whether the noun being replaced is masculine or feminine.

John sees it. [the book]

The book = **Il libro** is masculine singular.

Giovanni **lo** vede.
　　　　│
　direct object
　pronoun, masc. sing.

John sees it. [the car]

The car = **La macchina** is feminine singular.

Giovanni **la** vede.
　　　　│
　direct object
　pronoun, fem. sing.

John sees them. [the books]

The books = **I libri** is masculine plural.

Giovanni **li** vede.
　　　　│
　direct object
　pronoun, masc. pl.

John sees them. [the cars]

The cars = **Le macchine** is feminine plural.

Giovanni **le** vede.
　　　　│
　direct object
　pronoun, fem. pl.

- you (formal)

In the case of the singular formal *you,* note that the pronoun **La** refers to both a male and a female.

Sir, John sees you often.
Signore, Giovanni **La** vede spesso.

Mrs. Rossi, John sees you often.
Signora Rossi, Giovanni **La** vede spesso.

However, in the plural, the pronoun **Li** refers to males and **Le** to females.

Gentlemen, John sees you often.
Signori, Giovanni **Li** vede spesso.

Young ladies, John sees you often.
Signorine, Giovanni **Le** vede spesso.

2. <u>Indirect object pronouns</u>

1st pers. sing.	*to me*	mi
2nd pers.	*to you (fam.)*	ti
3rd pers.	⎧ *to him*	gli
	⎨ *to her*	le
	⎩ *to you (form. m. and f.)*	Le
1st pers. pl.	*to us*	ci
2nd pers.	*to you (fam.)*	vi
3rd pers.	⎧ *to them (m. and f.)*	loro
	⎨ *to you (form. m. and f.)*	Loro

The indirect object pronouns are used as they are in English, but, except for **loro,** they precede the conjugated verb.

The *to* preceding the English indirect object is not expressed in Italian when a pronoun is used; the Italian indirect object pronoun means *to me, to you,* etc.

- *John gives the book **to me**,* OR
  *John gives **me** the book.*

  John gives the book to whom? To me.
  To me is the indirect object.

  Giovanni **mi** da il libro.

  indirect object
  pronoun

- *John gives the book **to him**,* OR
  *John gives **him** the book.*

  John gives the book to whom? To him.
  To him is the indirect object.

  Giovanni **gli** da il libro.

  indirect object
  pronoun

- *John gives the book **to them**,* OR
  *John gives **them** the book.*

  John gives the book to whom? To them.
  To them is the indirect object.

  Giovanni da **loro** il libro.

  indirect object
  pronoun

As with the direct object pronouns, you will need to pay special attention to the equivalent of the English *you* (formal).

- you (formal)

In the case of the singular formal *you,* the pronoun **Le** refers to both a male and a female.

Sir (Madam),
*John is giving the book **to you**,* OR
*John is giving **you** the book.*

Signore (Signora),
Giovanni **Le** da il libro.

In the plural, **Loro** refers to both males and females.

Gentlemen (Young ladies),
*John is giving the book **to you**,* OR
*John is giving **you** the book.*

Signori (Signorine),
Giovanni da **Loro** il libro.

3. Object of preposition pronouns

1st pers. sing.	*for, with, etc. me*	me
2nd pers.	*for, with, etc. you (fam.)*	
3rd pers.	{ *for, with, etc. him*	lui
	for, with, etc. her	lei
	for, with, etc. you (form. m. and f.)	Lei
1st pers. pl.	*for, with, etc. us*	noi
2nd pers.	*for, with, etc. you (fam.)*	voi
3rd pers.	{ *for, with, etc. them (m. and f.)*	loro
	for, with, etc. you (form. m. and f.)	Loro

The object of preposition pronouns are used after a preposition other than the preposition *to.*

*Is the book for Paul? No, it is **for me.***

Me is the object of the preposition *for*.

È per Paolo il libro? No, è **per me.**

               object of preposition
               pronoun

*Are you going to the party with Mary? Yes, I'm going **with her.***

Her is the object of the preposition *with*.

Vai alla festa con Maria? Si, vado **con lei.**

               object of preposition
               pronoun

Do you have friends among the neighbors?
*Yes, we have friends **among them.***

Them is the object of the preposition *among*.

Avete amici tra i vicini?
Si, abbiamo amici **tra loro.**

               object of preposition
               pronoun

These forms of the pronoun are also used for emphasis or contrast in place of the direct or indirect object pronouns. In this function, they are called DISJUNCTIVE or STRESSED PRONOUNS and follow the verb, as opposed to the direct and indirect object pronouns, already treated in this chapter, which are called CONJUNCTIVE or UNSTRESSED PRONOUNS and usually precede the verb.

Compare the difference in meaning between the conjunctive (unstressed) and disjunctive (stressed) pronouns.

• Direct object

*I see **her**.* (unstressed)
La vedo.
|
conjunctive
direct object

*I see **her**.* (stressed—implying "I see her and no one else.")
Vedo **lei**.
|
disjunctive
direct object

*I see **her**, not **him**.* (contrast)
Vedo **lei**, non **lui**.
| |
disjunctive   disjunctive
direct object   direct object

• Indirect object

*I gave the book **to her**.* (unstressed)
Le ho dato il libro.
|
conjunctive
indirect object

*I gave the book **to her**.* (stressed—implying "I gave the book to her and no one else.")
Ho dato il libro **a lei**.
|
disjunctive
indirect object

*I gave the book **to her,** not **to them.*** (contrast)
Ho dato il libro **a lei,** non **a loro.**

disjunctive   disjunctive
indirect object   indirect object

Remember that some verbs in English take a preposition while the Italian equivalent does not and vice versa. Choose the pronoun according to its function in the Italian sentence (see p. 145).

Pronouns in summary:

Here is a chart of subject and object pronouns that we have studied so that you can readily compare the forms.

			Conjunctive		Disjunctive
		Subject	Direct Object	Indirect Object	Object of Preposition
S i n g u l a r	*1st pers.*	io	mi	mi	me
	2nd pers.	tu	ti	ti	te
	3rd pers.	lui lei Lei	lo la La	gli le Le	lui lei Lei
P l u r a l	*1st pers.*	noi	ci	ci	noi
	2nd pers.	voi	vi	vi	voi
	3rd pers.	loro Loro	li le Li Le	loro Loro	loro Loro

In order to choose the correct form of the pronoun for use in the Italian sentence follow these steps:

1. Determine the function of the pronoun in Italian.

   - Is it the subject?
   - Is it the direct object?
   - Is it the indirect object?
   - Is it the object of a preposition?
   - Is it a direct or an indirect object used for emphasis or contrast?

   In the case of the 3rd person also ask:

   - Does it replace a masculine or feminine noun?
   - Does it replace a singular or plural noun?

2. If there are two pronouns, one a direct object and one an indirect object:

   - Place them in the correct order, and make the necessary changes in form as indicated by your Italian textbook.

What is an Interrogative Pronoun?

An INTERROGATIVE PRONOUN is a word that replaces a noun and which introduces a question. Interrogative comes from *interrogate,* to question.

In English: Different interrogative pronouns are used for asking about persons and for asking about things.

1. ***Who, whom, whose,*** refer only to persons.

- ***who*** is used for the subject of the sentence.

    Who lives here?
    |
    subject

    Who are they?
    |
    subject

- ***whom*** is used for the direct object, indirect object, and object of preposition.

    Whom do you know here?
    |
    direct object

    To whom did you speak?
    |
    indirect object

    From whom did you get the book?
    |
    object of
    preposition

In colloquial English *who* is often used instead of *whom* and prepositions are placed at the end of the sentence, separated from the interrogative pronoun:

Who do you know here?
|
instead of *whom*

Who did you speak *to?*
|
preposition

Who did you get the book *from?*
|
preposition

- *whose* is the possessive form and is used to ask about possession or ownership.

I found a pencil. *Whose* is it?
|
possessive

They are nice cars. *Whose* are they?
|
possessive

2. *what* refers only to things and is used for subject, direct object, indirect object and object of preposition.

What happened?
|
subject

What do you want?
|
direct object

With *what* do you cook?

object of
preposition

3. ***which one, which ones*** refer to persons and things and are used when a choice is required. They may be used for subject, direct object, indirect object, and object of preposition.

All the teachers are here. *Which one* teaches Italian?

subject

I have two cars. *Which one* do you want to take?

direct object

There are many clerks here. With *which ones* did you want to speak?

object of
preposition

4. ***how much, how many*** refer to persons and things and are used to indicate quantity.

I have some money. *How much* do you want?

There were ten people present. *How many* voted in favor?

In Italian: As in English, different interrogative pronouns are used for asking about persons and for asking about things.

1. **chi** = *who, whom.* It refers only to persons. It is an invariable form and is used in all functions (subject, direct object, etc.) in the sentence.

Chi vive qui?
Who lives here?

Chi sono?
Who are they?

Chi conosci qui?
Whom do you know here?

The preposition must precede the interrogative pronoun **chi** when it is used as an indirect object or object of a preposition. It will therefore be necessary to restructure spoken English sentences.

Spoken English	Formal English
Who did you speak *to?* ⟶	*To whom* did you speak?
Who did you get the ⟶ book *from?*	*From whom* did you get the book?

The formal English word order is the only possible one in Italian.

A chi hai parlato?
To whom did you speak?

Da chi hai avuto il libro?
From whom did you get the book?

● **di chi** = *whose*

Restructure the English sentence replacing *whose* with *of whom.*

Whose is it? ⟶	**Of whom* is it?
Whose are they? ⟶	**Of whom* are they?

Di chi è?
Whose is it?

---

*An asterisk indicates that the sentence is ungrammatical.

Di chi sono?
Whose are they?

2. **che** = *what*. It refers only to things. It is an invariable form and is used in all functions in the sentence.

Che è successo?
What happened?

Che vuoi?
What do you want?

Con **che** cucini?
With what do you cook?

Che cosa and **cosa** are used interchangeably with **che** with no difference in meaning.

3. **quale, quali** = *which one, which ones*. It refers to both persons and things. It has singular and plural forms to agree in number with the noun it replaces and is used in all functions in the sentence.

Ci sono due insegnanti qui.
There are two teachers here.

Quale insegna italiano?
Which one teaches Italian?

Ho due macchine.
I have two cars.

Quale vuoi prendere?
Which one do you want to take?

Ci sono molti impiegati qui.
There are many clerks here.

Con **quali** voleva parlare?
With which ones did you want to speak?

Since the question *what is. . . ?* or *what are. . . ?* can be translated into Italian by either **che + essere. . . ?** or **quale, quali + essere. . . ?** notice the following:

- **che + essere...?** is used when the expected answer is a definition.

  What is poetry?

  > The expected answer is a definition of poetry.
  > Therefore, **che è** is used for *what is...?*

  Che è la poesia?

- **quale, quali + essere...?** is used when the expected answer provides one of a number of possible answers.

  What is your favorite novel?

  > The expected answer will indicate which novel
  > (of those written) is the favorite one.
  > Therefore, **quale** is used for *what is...?*

  Quale è il tuo romanzo preferito?

  When in doubt, if the *what* of the English sentence can be replaced by *which one(s),* then use **quale, quali** in Italian.

4. **quanto (-a, -i, -e)** = *how much, how many.* The singular forms **quanto, quanta** refer to things and the plural **quanti, quante** refer to both persons and things. It has four forms to agree in gender and number with the noun it replaces. It is used in all functions in the sentence.

Ho del denaro.   **Quanto** vuoi?
masc. sing.   masc. sing.

I have some money.   *How much do you want?*

C'erano dieci studenti presenti.   **Quanti** hanno votato a favore?
masc. pl.   masc. pl.

There were ten students present. How many voted in favor?

What is a Demonstrative Pronoun?

A DEMONSTRATIVE PRONOUN is a word that replaces a noun which has been pointed out. Demonstrative comes from *demonstrate*, to point out.

In English: The singular demonstrative pronouns are *this (one)* and *that (one);* the plural forms are *these* and *those.*

This suitcase is big and that suitcase is small.

demonstrative   demonstrative
adjective   adjective

This (one) is big and *that (one)* is small.

demonstrative   demonstrative
pronoun   pronoun

These suitcases are big and those suitcases are small.

demonstrative   demonstrative
adjective   adjective

These are big and *those* are small.

demonstrative   demonstrative
pronoun   pronoun

As with the demonstrative adjectives, *this (one)/these* refer to a person or an object near the speaker and *that (one)/those* to a person or an object away from the speaker.

In Italian: The demonstrative pronouns are the same as the demonstrative adjectives: **questo (-a, -i, -e)** and **quello (-a, -i, -e).**

As pronouns, they will replace the demonstrative adjective + noun; they will therefore agree in gender and number with the noun replaced.

1. Forms used to point out a person or an object near the speaker:

questo (-a, -i, -e) = *this (one), these*

Identify the gender and number of the noun replaced and choose the form that agrees with it.

- *Which book do you want?* ***This one.***

  Noun replaced: *book (***libro)**
  Gender, number: masculine singular
  Therefore, *this one* = **questo**

  Quale libro vuoi? **Questo.**

- *Which houses did you build?* ***These.***

  Noun replaced: *houses* **(case)**
  Gender, number: feminine plural
  Therefore, *these* = **queste**

  Quali case hai costruito? **Queste.**

2. Forms used to point out a person or an object away from the speaker:

quello (-a, -i, -e) = *that (one), those*

When used as a pronoun, **quello** has only these four forms; not all of the additional forms of the demonstrative adjective.

- *Which book do you want?* ***That one.***

  Noun replaced: *book* **(libro)**
  Gender, number: masculine singular
  Therefore, *that one* = **quello**

  Quale libro vuoi? **Quello.**

- *Which houses did you build? **Those.***

    Noun replaced: *houses* **(case)**
    Gender, number: feminine plural
    Therefore, *those* = **quelle**

    Quali case hai costruito? **Quelle.**

Quello (-a, -i, -e) is also used to translate the English pronouns, *the one/the ones,* followed by an adverb, a prepositional phrase or a relative clause (see **What is a Relative Pronoun?**, p. 169) which give additional information about the nouns to which they refer.

- *Which book do you want? **The one** over there.*

    <u>over there</u>
    adverb
    Quale libro vuoi? **Quello** la.

- *Which book do you want? **The one** on the table.*

    <u>on the table</u>
    prepositional phrase
    Quale libro vuoi? **Quello** sul tavolo.

- *Which books do you want? **The ones** that I gave you.*

    <u>that I gave you</u>
    relative clause
    Quali libri vuoi? **Quelli** che ti ho dato.

There is another common use of the pronoun **quello (-a, -i, -e)** with the meaning *the one/the ones.*

• *Which house are you selling? My father's.*

The only way of expressing in Italian the distinctly English construction *my father's* is to change it to **the one of my father* and then translate *the one* with the proper form of **quello.**

> my father's ———▶*the one of my father

The one refers to the noun it replaces, *house.*
The Italian equivalent for *house* (**casa**) is feminine singular.
Therefore, use feminine singular form of demonstrative pronoun: **quella.**

Quale casa vendete? **Quella di mio padre.**

• *Which pens are you using? My brother's.*

> my brother's ———▶ *the ones of my brother

The ones refers to the noun it replaces, *pens.*
The Italian equivalent for *pens* (**penne**) is feminine plural.
Therefore, use feminine plural form of demonstrative pronoun: **quelle.**

Quali penne usi? **Quelle di mio fratello.**

Constructions such as *my father's, my brother's,* etc., must always be reworked as shown above before they can be translated into Italian.

---

*An asterisk indicates that what follows is ungrammatical or awkward.

What is a Possessive Pronoun?

A POSSESSIVE PRONOUN is a word that replaces a noun and which indicates the possessor of that noun. Possessive comes from *possess,* to own.

I'm reading my magazines; you are reading *yours.*

Yours is a pronoun which replaces the noun, *magazines,* and which indicates the possessor of that noun, *you.*

In English: Here is a list of the possessive pronouns:

> mine
> yours
> his, hers, its
> ours
> yours
> theirs

The possessive pronoun refers only to the possessor and has no grammatical relationship with the noun being replaced.

Example 1. Is that your house? Yes, it is *mine.*

Example 2. Are those your keys? Yes, they are *mine.*

The same possessive pronoun *mine* is used, although the object possessed is singular in Example 1 *(house)* and plural in Example 2 *(keys).*

In Italian: The possessive pronoun refers to the possessor and, in addition, must agree in gender and number with the noun it replaces. The forms of the possessive pronoun are identical to the forms of the possessive adjective, and they must be used with the definite article (see p. 116).

168

- Io leggo le mie riviste; tu leggi **le tue.**

  Le tue refers to the possessor **(tu),** but agrees in gender and number with the noun being replaced **(riviste).**

  I am reading my magazines; you are reading **yours.**

- Noi vediamo spesso le nostre sorelle; voi non vedete **le vostre.**

  Le vostre refers to the possessor **(voi),** but agrees in gender and number with the noun being replaced **(sorelle).**

  We see our sisters often; you don't see **yours.**

As you can see from the above examples, not only are the forms of the possessive pronoun identical to those of the possessive adjective, but the use of them as well. From a practical point of view, it is a simple matter of not repeating the noun which the pronoun is replacing. It will help you, therefore, to review the chapter **What is a Possessive Adjective?, p. 115.**

What is a Relative Pronoun?

A RELATIVE PRONOUN is a pronoun that serves two purposes:

1. As a pronoun it stands for a noun or another pronoun previously mentioned (called its ANTECEDENT). The antecedent is part of the MAIN CLAUSE; that is, a group of words containing a subject and a verb expressing a complete thought.

> This is the boy *who* broke the window.
>
>   antecedent
>   noun

> It is he *who* broke the window.
>
>   antecedent
>   pronoun

2. It introduces a SUBORDINATE CLAUSE; that is, a group of words containing a subject and a verb (separate from the subject and verb of the main clause) not expressing a complete thought.

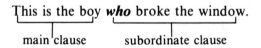

>   main clause   subordinate clause

The above subordinate clause is also called a RELATIVE CLAUSE and starts with a relative pronoun *(who)*. The relative pronoun relates the subordinate clause to its antecedent *(boy)* and gives us additional information about him.

In English and in Italian the choice of the appropriate relative pronoun will depend on its function in the relative clause. You will need to go through the following steps:

1. Identify the relative clause.

2. Identify the relative pronoun.

3. Identify the antecedent; what word in the main clause does the relative pronoun relate to?

4. Determine the function of the relative pronoun within the relative clause.

   - Is it the subject?
   - Is it the direct object?
   - Is it the indirect object?
   - Is it an object of a preposition?
   - Is it a possessive modifier?

5. Select the pronoun according to its antecedent.

   - Is it a person?
   - Is it a thing?

In English: Here are the English relative pronouns.

Subject of the relative clause

- **who** (if the antecedent is a person)

   This is the student *who* answered.
   |
   antecedent

   Who is the subject of *answered.*

- **which** (if the antecedent is a thing)

   This is the book *which* is so popular.
   |
   antecedent

   Which is the subject of *is.*

• *that* (if the antecedent is a person or a thing)

She is the only student *that* answers all the time.
|
antecedent

That is the subject of *answers.*

This is the book *that* is so popular.
|
antecedent

That is the subject of *is.*

Object of the relative clause: These pronouns are often omitted in English. We have indicated them in parentheses because they must be expressed in Italian.

• *whom* (if the antecedent is a person)

This is the student *(whom)* I saw yesterday.
| |
antecedent   subject of relative clause

Whom is the direct object of *saw.*

• *which* (if the antecedent is a thing)

This is the book *(which)* I bought.
| |
antecedent   subject of relative clause

Which is the direct object of *bought.*

• *that* (if the antecedent is a person or thing)

She is the only student *(that)* I saw.
| |
antecedent   subject of relative clause

That is the direct object of *saw.*

This is the book *(that)* I read.

antecedent   subject of relative clause

That is the direct object of *read.*

Indirect object of the relative clause

• *whom* (if the antecedent is a person)

Here is the student *to whom* I was speaking.

antecedent   subject of relative clause

To whom is the indirect object of *was speaking.*

The above is an example of formal English sentence structure. Spoken English, however, often omits the relative pronoun and places the preposition at the end of the sentence; this is called a DANGLING PREPOSITION.

Here is the student I was speaking *to.*

The spoken English sentence structure cannot be translated into Italian since Italian always requires that the relative pronoun be expressed and that a preposition always be followed by its object. The formal English structure will give you the correct Italian structure.

Spoken English	Formal English
Here is the student ⟶ I am speaking *to.*	Here is the student *to whom* I am speaking.

• **which** (when the antecedent is a thing)

Here is the museum *to which* he gave a painting.

    antecedent   subject of relative clause

To which is the indirect object of *gave*.

In spoken English:

Here is the museum he gave the painting *to*.

Object of preposition of the relative clause

• **whom** (if the antecedent is a person)

Here is the student *about whom* I was speaking.

    antecedent   subject of relative clause

Whom is the object of the preposition *about*.

As in the case of the indirect object, spoken English often omits the relative pronoun and places the preposition at the end of the sentence.

Here is the student I was speaking *about*.

Again, only the formal English structure will give you the correct Italian structure.

Spoken English	Formal English
Here is the student I was speaking *about*. ⟶	Here is the student *about whom* I was speaking.

- *which* (if the antecedent is a thing)

This is the book *about which* I was speaking.
        antecedent   subject of relative clause

Which is the object of the preposition *about*.

In spoken English:

This is the book I was speaking *about*.

Possessive modifier

- *whose* (if the antecedent is a person)

Here is the woman *whose* car was stolen.
      antecedent
             possessive modifying *car*

Relative clauses are a very common type of clause. We use them in our everyday speech without giving much thought to why and how we construct them. The relative pronoun of these clauses allows us to relate in a single sentence two thoughts which have a common element (a noun or a pronoun).

Let us look at a few examples of how we construct relative clauses:

- Sentence A: The students passed the exam.
  Sentence B: The students studied.

The common element here is the noun *students*. To combine the two sentences A and B in one and avoid repetition of the noun *student*, we normally use a relative pronoun which immediately follows its antecedent.

The students *who* studied passed the exam.
    antecedent relative clause

- Sentence A: The man was embarrassed.
  Sentence B: We were talking about the man.

The common element here is the noun *man*. To combine the two sentences A and B in one and avoid repetition of the noun *man* we normally use a relative pronoun preceded by the preposition *about,* of which it is the object.

The man *about whom* we were talking was embarrassed.

    antecedent   relative clause

In spoken English the relative pronoun is normally omitted:

The man we were talking about was embarrassed.

    antecedent   relative clause

In Italian: To determine the correct relative pronoun in Italian, you must go through the following steps:

1. Identify the relative clause; restructure the English clause if there is a dangling preposition.

2. Identify the antecedent; what word in the main clause does the relative clause relate to?

3. Determine the function of the relative pronoun within the relative clause:

   Is it the subject, direct object, indirect object, object of preposition, or possessive modifier?

There are fewer relative pronouns than in English and the choice of a relative pronoun depends only on its function in the relative clause. Italian uses one pronoun for subject and direct object and another one for indirect object and object of preposition.

Subject/object of the relative clause

che = *who/whom/that/which*

Che is invariable and can be used as subject or object of a relative clause; it can refer to persons or things.

- *The students who studied passed the exam.*

  subject of
  relative clause

  Gli studenti **che** hanno studiato hanno superato l'esame.

- *This is the student (whom) I saw yesterday.*

  direct object of
  relative clause

  Questo è lo studente **che** ho visto ieri.

- *Here is the book (that) I bought.*
  Here is the book (which) I bought.

  direct object of
  relative clause

  Ecco il libro **che** ho comprato.

Indirect object/object of a preposition in the relative clause

PREPOSITION + **cui** = *to whom/to which* or *about, of, from,* etc. + *whom/which*

Cui is invariable and can be used as indirect object (after the preposition **a**) or as the object of any other preposition; it can refer to persons or things.

- *Here is the student I was speaking to.*

- *Here is the student to whom I was speaking.*

  indirect object of
  relative clause

  Ecco lo studente **a cui** parlavo.

- *These are the books I was speaking about.*

- *These are the books about which I was speaking.*

  object of preposition
  in relative clause

  Questi sono i libri **di cui** parlavo.

Possessive modifier

DEFINITE ARTICLE + **cui** = *whose*

cui is invariable but the definite article must agree in gender and number with the noun it modifies (the person or item possessed) which immediately follows **cui.**

- *Here is the woman **whose** son won the prize.*

  possessor   person possessed

  Ecco la donna **il cui** figlio ha vinto il premio.

  masc. sing. masc. sing.

- *Here is the woman **whose** pearls were stolen.*

  possessor   item possessed

  Ecco la donna **le cui** perle sono state rubate.

  fem. pl.   fem. pl.

What are Relative Pronouns without Antecedents?

The RELATIVE PRONOUNS without antecedents refer to an antecedent which is either not expressed or is a whole idea, not a specific noun or pronoun.

In English: The relative pronoun *what* meaning *that which* occurs without an antecedent.

Compare these sentences:

Here is the book *(that)* I read.

antecedent of *that:* book

Here is *what* I read.

no antecedent

I don't know *what* happened.

no antecedent

The relative pronoun *which* refers back to a whole idea, not a specific noun or pronoun.

Compare these sentences:

Here is the book *(which)* I read.

antecedent of *which:*
book

You speak many languages, *which* is an asset nowadays.

antecedent of *which:*
you speak many languages

She didn't do well on the test, *which* I didn't expect at all.

antecedent of *which:*
she didn't do well on the test

In Italian: The relative pronouns **quello che** and **ciò che** meaning *what (that which)* also occur without an antecedent. They are invariable in form and can function as subject or object.

Non so $\begin{cases} \textbf{quello che} \\ \textbf{ciò che} \end{cases}$ è successo.

*I don't know **what** happened.*

Ecco $\begin{cases} \textbf{quello che} \\ \textbf{ciò che} \end{cases}$ ho letto.

*Here is **what** I read.*

The relative pronoun **il che** refers back to a whole idea. It is invariable in form and can function as subject or object.

Parli molte lingue, **il che** è un vantaggio oggigiorno.
*You speak many languages, **which** is an asset nowadays.*

Non ha fatto bene all'esame, **il che** non mi aspettavo affatto.
*She didn't do well on the test, **which** I didn't expect at all.*

What are Indefinites and Negatives?

INDEFINITES are words which refer to persons, things or periods of time which are not specific or which are not clearly defined.

In English: Some common indefinites are *someone, anybody, something, some day.* The indefinites are frequently paired with negatives and for convenience these words are often learned as pairs of opposites.

Indefinites		Negatives
someone anyone	≠	no one
somebody anybody	≠	nobody
something anything	≠	nothing
some day any day	≠	never

Is *anyone* coming tonight? *No one.*

Does *anybody* live here? *Nobody.*

Do you have *anything* for me? *Nothing.*

Are you going to Europe *some day? Never.*

English sentences use the word *not* to become negative. (See **What are Affirmative and Negative Sentences?**, p. 45.)

I am studying.
I am *not* studying.

In addition, the negative words can also make a statement negative.

> *No one* is coming.
> He has *never* seen a movie.

English allows only one negative word in a sentence (or clause). If the word *not* appears, another negative word cannot be used in that same sentence.

> *I am *not* studying *nothing*.

This sentence contains a double negative: *not* and *nothing*. It is incorrect English.

The indefinite word which is the opposite of the negative word is used in sentences containing *not*.

> I am *not* studying *anything*.

Here is another example.

> I have *nothing*.
> *Nothing* is the one negative word.

> I do *not* have *anything*.
> The sentence contains *not;* therefore,
> the word *anything* is substituted for
> *nothing*.

> * I do *not* have *nothing*.
> This sentence contains a double negative—
> *not* and *nothing*—and is incorrect English.

---

*An asterisk before a sentence means that the sentence is ungrammatical.

In Italian: As in English, the indefinites and negatives exist as pairs of opposites.

Indefinites		Negatives	
something ⎫ *anything* ⎭	qualcosa	niente, nulla	*nothing*
everything	tutto		
some, any	qualche, alcuno	nessuno	⎰*no one,* ⎱*not any*
someone/somebody ⎫ *anyone/anybody* ⎭	qualcuno	nessuno	⎰*no one,* ⎱*nobody*
everyone/everybody	tutti		
always *sometimes*	sempre qualche volta	mai	*never*
also, too	anche	neanche	*not...either*
either, or	o	né	*neither*
either...or	o...o	né...né	*neither...nor*

Contrary to English, in Italian the indefinites cannot appear in a negative sentence. If the verb is preceded by **non** *(not)*, an indefinite cannot be used in the same sentence. Instead, a negative is used.

<table>
<tr><td align="center">English</td><td align="center">Italian</td></tr>
</table>

not + indefinite word   ⟶   **non** + negative word

*I do **not** have **anything**.*
    | |
   not   indefinite word

Non ho **niente**.
 | |
not   negative word *(nothing)*

In order to use the indefinites and negatives correctly in Italian it will often be necessary to reword the English sentence so that *not* will be followed by a negative word, the opposite of the English indefinite.

> I do *not* see *anybody.*———►*I do *not* see *nobody.*

Then express in Italian:

Non vedo **nessuno.**

Let's look at some other examples.

- *I do **not** want to eat **anything.***

  1. Locate the indefinite: anything
  2. Decide what the opposite of the English indefinite is: anything ——► nothing
  3. Transform the English sentence using a double negative: *I do not want to eat nothing.
  4. Put the sentence into Italian.

Non voglio mangiare **niente.**

- *I don't (do **not**) have **any** intention of doing that.*

  1. Locate the indefinite: any
  2. Decide what the opposite of the English indefinite is: any ——► no
  3. Transform the English sentence using a double negative: *I don't have *no* intention of doing that.
  4. Put the sentence into Italian.

Non ho **nessuna** intenzione di farlo.

---

*An asterisk means that what follows is ungrammatical.

Index